# THE NEW PREDATOR:
# WOMEN WHO KILL

## Profiles of Female Serial Killers

# Dr. Deborah Schurman-Kauflin

# THE NEW PREDATOR: WOMEN WHO KILL

## PROFILES OF FEMALE SERIAL KILLERS

Algora Publishing
New York

Algora Publishing, New York
© 2000 by Algora Publishing
All rights reserved. Published 2000.
Printed in the United States of America
ISBN: 1-892941-58-9
Editors@algora.com


Library of Congress Cataloging-in-Publication Data 00-011035

Schurman-Kauflin, Deborah S.
  The new predator: women who kill,  Profiles of female serial killers /
By Deborah S. Schurman-Kauflin.
      p. cm.
Includes bibliographical records.
  ISBN 1-892941-58-9 (alk. paper)
  1.  Women serial murderers—United States—Psychology. 2.  Criminal
Behavior—Research—Methodology. 3.  Criminal methods—Research—
Methodology—Case studies.  I. Title: Profiles of female serial killers. II. Title.
  HV6529 .S34 2000
  364.15'23'0820973--dc21
                    00-011035

New York
www.algora.com

TABLE OF CONTENTS

*Introduction*

Why is so little known about women who kill? What drives them? How do they operate? Are they the same as male murderers, or do they (and the crimes they commit) differ in critical ways?

The number of unsolved homicides and unclassified murders has steadily increased, and we need better information and better tools in order to unravel these perplexing cases — and, hopefully, to help prevent new ones. This study on female multicide is intended to provide at least partial answers to some of the fundamental questions, and to indicate some of the areas that still remain to be investigated.

Existing literature on the phenomenon of female-perpetrated multicide does provide basic profiles of the women and their crimes, but until now, most research has concentrated on male offenders. This book is an in-depth study of females convicted of multiple murder in the United States and is, we believe, the first to be based on direct in-person interviews with the women themselves. Thus it offers invaluable insights that have never before been available to law enforcement professionals, counselors, and others who are concerned with convicted or potential offenders.

Prior research conducted by the F.B.I. has examined commonalities in the backgrounds of male multiple murderers through in-depth interviews with male offenders. The results of the F.B. I. study have proven useful in criminal investigations. However, until this writing, female multiple murderers had not been studied in the same way.

Therefore, a sample of females convicted of multiple homicide was interviewed to determine whether similarly helpful data could be gathered. The goal was to generate a profile of the female offender, and the research questions aimed at determining whether there were any telling commonalities in the lives of female multiple murderers. This research is unique.

Females convicted of multicide are a rare breed. Thus, there were few incarcerated offenders to examine. The study involved in-depth, face-to-face interviews with seven of them: four serial killers and three mass murderers. The author conducted the interviews with the convicted murderers, and the interviews varied in duration from 2 ½ to 7 hours. The interviews were the primary data source, although trial transcripts, pre-sentencing reports, and other sources were used as well.

The results provide a profile of the female multiple murderer. Like their male counterparts, female killers endured patterns of extreme emotional, physical, and sexual abuse as children. Due to the familial turmoil the female offender, like the male multiple murderer, turned inward to an introverted fantasy life. Isolation became a way of life, and contact with others became less frequent. It appears that violence emerges from violence, whether the violence is physical, emotional, or sexual.

# 1.

## MURDER

> "I never understood my capacity for compassion until I started killing."
>
> *— a female convicted of 5 murders*

What makes a person kill? What is it that drives a living human being to take the life of another? This troubling query has plagued societies since the beginning of time. Poignant to all social strata, homicide is a mystery to both the poor and the wealthy, the young and the old, women and men. Every type of person can be a killer, no matter what background, race or gender, and this is what makes killing so puzzling. The phenomenon challenges every nation, and almost every notion (from greed and lust to envy and anger) has been proposed as reasons why human beings destroy one another, yet no one of them is a solid explanation, the single key that would unlock the enigma. The question persists: why do people kill?

Throughout the annals of time, people have continually stepped into a duo — the combination of predator and prey — in a never-ending cycle of life and death. Every government and every people faces macabre episodes of inexplicable rage and violence. Yet the United States holds the dubious distinction of having the highest number of killers on Earth. Nearly 20,000 people are murdered each year in the U.

S. (*Sourcebook of Criminal Justice*, 1997). This number has grown over time despite governmental efforts at rehabilitation and deterrence, and, frighteningly, there is one particular aspect of homicide that has steadily increased: unsolved homicides, unclassified murders.

Unsolved cases are weights that drag down homicide detectives over the course of their careers, despite efforts to push them aside, to forget them. Like a far-off telephone, these irritating cases are waiting, still waiting to be answered. With new and better forensic techniques being developed every day, one has to ask how the number of unsolvable murders can still increase. This question cycles back to the foundation of homicide, the inquiry of why people kill.

In an effort to better understand homicide and in an attempt to decrease unsolved homicides, researchers have tried to create composites of individuals who commit acts of murder. The notion was that if we could understand who is committing the crimes then we could discover why they were acting out.

Preliminary results have been both informative and, at the same time, misleading (always a risk with generalities). Such studies have concentrated on the offenders and their personal characteristics at the time of their crimes, and what research has shown is that most killers tend to be young males who emerge from lower socioeconomic areas. On closer inspection, it was found that such individuals tend to be filled with rage over traumatic childhoods, and the typical act of homicide is a product of an explosion of anger or a fight. Such crimes are more easily solved because most often, in explosive homicides, the killer and victim know each other (Geberth, 1998).

So, if the typical homicide involves an explosion of anger or a fight in which victim and perpetrator are well acquainted, then how can solvability be decreasing? The simple answer involves the nature of victim and killer; that relationship has changed over time. In the last fifty years, one of the most disturbing trends in homicide has been the increase in stranger-perpetrated violence, including the headline-snatching phenomena of serial and mass murder.

Of the nearly 20,000 murders in the United States every year, there are no exact figures for how many of them were committed by serial killers. Why is that? The primary explanation is that it is difficult to determine the number of serial killers who are active at any one time because there is no one clear definition of the term. There are almost as many definitions of serial killing as there are researchers, and so it is difficult to designate who fits the category of serial offender.

Serial murder has been defined as "two or more separate murders where an individual, acting alone or with another, commits multiple homicides over a period of time, with time breaks between each murder event." (Geberth, 1996: 438). Keeney and Heide (1994: 384) define serial murder as the "premeditated murder of three or more victims committed over time, in separate incidents, in a civilian context, with the murder activity being chosen by the offender." Hickey (1991) simply defines serial murder as killing over time. Holmes and Holmes (1994: 92) define a serial killer as "someone who murders at least three persons in more than a thirty-day period." Serial murder has also been defined as "one person killing another in the context of power, control, sexuality, and aggressive brutality" (Burgess et al., 1986: 252); and as the killing of victims on different occasions (Levin & Fox, 1985). As the *crème de la crème*, Dietz (1986) suggests that in order to be a serial killer, one must kill 10 people in 10 or more separate incidents.

Egger (1997: 5) defines serial murder as occurring when:

(1) One or more individuals [in many cases, males] commit (s) a second murder and/or subsequent murder; (2) there is generally no prior relationship between victim and attacker

(if there is a relationship, such a relationship will place the victim in a subjugated role to the killer); (3) subsequent murders are at different times and have no apparent connection to the initial murder; and (4) are usually committed in a different geographical location. Further, (5) the motive is not material gain but the murderer's desire to have power or dominance over his victims. (6) Victims may have symbolic value for the murderer and/or are perceived to be without prestige and, in most instances, are unable to defend themselves or alert others to their plight, or are perceived as powerless given their situation in time, place, or status within their immediate surroundings. Examples include (7) vagrants, the homeless, prostitutes, migrant workers, homosexuals, missing children, single women [out by themselves], elderly women, college students, and hospital patients.

After reviewing the various definitions, it becomes obvious why it is so difficult to estimate how many serial killers are operating in the United States, much less to gather any more detailed data on the topic. For the purposes of the current study, we are defining serial killers as those who murder two or more victims, with an emotional cooling-off period between the homicides, and mass murderers as those who kill five or more victims, with no emotional cooling-off period between homicides.

What researchers do agree upon is the fact that most serial killers prey upon strangers, and this is what contributes to homicide insolvability (Holmes & Holmes, 1998). Because stranger-perpetrated violence is on the rise (as is the number of unsolved homicides), and since serial killers typically select unknown victims, it becomes very important to analyze the serial killers in order to develop comprehension of the offenders and their crimes. Simply stated, if law enforcement officials have a better comprehension of the offenders and their patterns, there is an increased opportunity to solve what would otherwise be unsolvable homicides. It is far more difficult to solve a murder when victim and assailant are not familiar with each other, so having background composites of offenders who tend to choose unknown victims provides police with an indispensable and effective tool to aid in their criminal investigations.

When looking at that twin, serial murder-mass murder, there seems at first to be little connection to unsolved murders. That is, those who commit mass murders are usually apprehended by police.

It is common to confuse the terms "serial murder" and "mass murder," mainly because the popular media use the terms interchangeably, yet they are different crimes and are committed in diverse ways. Mass murder involves the killing of several people in one instance. Unlike the elusive serial killer, the mass killer is one who seems to explode and kill in public places, taking the lives of several people at once. Mass murderers kill many victims, but they do so as part of one single plan. The killings are not separate and thus there is no emotional cooling-off period between the homicides. The key point to remember is that the mass killer does not cool down and reflect upon each homicide before taking another life. Instead, these murderers kill one victim and then proceed directly to another as part of one emotional thought process. All of the killings are directly related.

Mass murderer Charles Whitman vividly demonstrates this point. In 1966, Whitman shot 46 people, killing 16, in Austin, Texas after ascending the tower at the University of Texas and shooting at anyone on the ground. Most people are unaware of the fact that the day prior to the shooting, Whitman killed his mother in her home and then proceeded to his own home where he killed his wife (Holmes & Holmes, 1994). Obviously Mr. Whitman did not "cool off" between the homicides. This was all part of a single plan for Whitman, albeit it a plan spread over more than one day and more than one location.

So there is a distinction between serial and mass killings, despite the fact that both kill many victims. Though the mass murder often involves injuries to strangers ("stranger-perpetrated homicide"), in most instances this type of killer either commits suicide at the crime scene, or attempts suicide by cop (in which the perpetrator tries to incite police to shoot and kill him), or the offender voluntarily gives himself up. Thus, solving mass murders is typically easier for police than investigating a serial killer who preys upon unrelated victims and then melds back into society, making every attempt to blend back into the mainstream. This makes the process of capturing a serial offender much more difficult than catching a mass killer.

**What Do We Know?**

Research has shown that male *mass* murderers tend to use overt methods, including guns, to kill their victims; and the scant research on female mass murderers indicates that they use guns as well. Male *serial* killers, too, use overt murder methods such as bludgeoning, stabbing, and strangling. But *female serial killers* typically kill using covert methods such as suffocation or poisoning.

The F.B.I.'s research into commonalities in the backgrounds of male multiple murderers through in-depth interviews indicate an offender dichotomy. Simply stated, male serial killers tend to fall into one of two categories, either "organized" or "disorganized." Each category has background characteristics and commonalities that are indicative of the dichotomy. From the F.B.I.'s studies, "organized" offenders plan their offenses and leave little evidence. "Disorganized" offenders commit spontaneous homicides, which indicate little planning.

Unsurprisingly, the United States holds the most multiple murderers in the world (this follows, since the U.S. has the most murders overall). Historically, the bulk of the research regarding such crimes has been concentrated in the U.S. Groundbreaking projects have analyzed male multiple murderers and how they go about committing their heinous crimes. The deciphering of these offenders was thought to enable law enforcement to predict behavior.

Criminologists, psychologists, and sociologists have proposed several classifications of these killers after conducting in-person interviews to gain cognitive insight into the mental meanderings of perpetrators who select multiple victims. Resulting from these studies was a composite of the personalities and patterns involving victim selection, method of murder, and body disposal (Ressler, et al., 1988). Now, by studying convicted criminals, law enforcement can analyze criminal actions (how the offender kills) and accordingly predict future behavior. This is known as profiling.

Catching a multiple murderer is a daunting task for law enforcement because specialized knowledge is essential to understand the motivations that guide individuals who commit these crimes. In order to predict what an offender will do, a law enforcement officer must grasp the mentality of one who kills. To do this, the officer must look beyond physical evidence and examine the behaviors that are present at a crime scene.

Profiling is a tool that allows experts to create a personal composite of someone who has committed a crime. This profile is based on years of study, homicide investigations, research, and recognition of patterns. Whether a profiler gives tips on the type of person who would be a suspect, or whether the profiler predicts offender behavior, the benefits of using an expert can be essential to the successful apprehension of a multiple murderer. Because the U.S. has the highest number of such offenders, every forensic tool available must be utilized.

However, the existing knowledge base is exclusionary — it does not contain data on female multiple killers. And this is where the current research comes in. Chapter 3 analyzes females based on this author's interviews with female offenders. Profiles have been created and can be directly applied in criminal investigations.

**Female Serial Killers**

At any one time it is estimated that there are between 50-75 serial killers operating in the United States. Of this number, approximately 7-8 are female, which is consistent with studies on murder in general, where women comprise only a small percentage of those who kill (Hickey, 1997).

Yet there has been a startling trend in the last thirty years, a trend that potentially affects everyone, young and old, male and female. *One third* of all recorded female serial killers began their murderous activities since 1970 (Hickey, 1991). Broken down, this means that there have been over 26 female serial killers within the United States in the last thirty years (author's files). This is a huge increase in the latter part of the 20th century, and strangely, the media have ignored the phenomenon. Growing like a plague of locusts, these female predators prey upon the elderly and the infirm, making almost anyone a potential target.

The early 1980's saw the likes of Christine Falling, was who convicted of killing three children whom she was babysitting — and she freely admits to killing three more. In 1988, Dorothea Puente was convicted of killing nine elderly boarders by poisoning them. In the late 1980's, Bobbie Sue Terrell was convicted of killing two of her hospital patients by injecting a drug into an IV, but she is suspected in many other deaths. Nurse Beverly Allit was convicted of killing four children and attempting to kill nine others in 1993. The late 1990's brought the arrest of Kathleen Anne Atkinson, who was linked with the death of two young girls and two elderly women. And the list continues with more being added each year.

Because this phenomenon has been ignored, by and large law enforcement agencies, as well as society as a whole, fail to realize that females can and do commit acts of multiple murder. And because police are not knowledgeable about these killers, it is far more likely that the killers can go undetected. Female serial killers murder their victims in plain view, for the entire world to see. But typically, no one believes that a woman could kill multiple victims, so the deaths are categorized as undetermined or unsolved. This is exactly why female multiple murderers can be considered more dangerous than male offenders: females can kill without anyone knowing what they are doing, and without anyone stopping them.

**What Better Way to Kill?**

Perhaps even more disturbing than the pittance of offender information is the disbelief that surrounds female serial killers. Very few people believe that a female could hold the vicious capacity to commit serial murder, despite confessions from the offenders themselves. For example, in Michigan, two women were convicted of killing nursing home patients within their care by smothering them. In a macabre game, they decided to spell out the word "murder" with the names of the victims whom they killed. Gwen Graham and Cathy Wood eventually had difficulty killing a lady named "Ursula," and finally decided to give up their amusement (Fox & Levin, 1994). Cathy Wood described the crimes in detail to police, but to this day, many refuse to believe that she and her accomplice could commit such atrocious acts.

Along those same lines, in June 1999, Pittsburgh, Pennsylvania resident Marie Noe plea-bargained her way to probation after admitting to the killings of her 8 children. It has been suggested that her 72-year-old appearance and her gender affected the decision not to place what can only be categorized as a serial killer in prison. The fact that someone could kill 8 people in the United States and receive probation is unacceptable and frightening. Imagine giving any other killer a "Get 8 Murders Free" card. This concept is unimaginable, but that is exactly what Pittsburgh did with Ms. Noe. Well-known convicted serial killers Lawrence Bittker and Roy Norris were connected with the deaths of five young women. Should we let them out? After all, five is less than eight.

Obviously, public opinion dictates prosecutions in these cases, so when society is unfamiliar with these killers and is reluctant to believe that women kill serially, it makes obtaining a conviction much more difficult and leads to lack-luster investigations and lack of prosecution. It is all a matter of perception, and until the public realizes what a danger female predators present, essentially, a free pass for killing is offered to those females who choose to engage in this behavior. If nothing is done, more and more females will take advantage of that. The question is, when will one of these newest predators touch your life?

Faced with the growing numbers of female killers, one may ask why law enforcement agencies know so little about these killers and their methods. If we look at the existing information concerning these offenders, the answer becomes simple: law enforcement agencies lack the information because very little information has been gathered. But if the numbers of female serial killers are increasing so dramatically, then why isn't there a wealth of information?

First, they are still relatively few, compared to the number of male killers; and second, female serial killers are hesitant to discuss their crimes. Having interviewed both male and female serial killers, this author can attest to the fact that males more readily grant interviews while females remain reticent to speak. This has made in-depth analysis of these women virtually impossible until now.

Thirdly, women have been traditionally viewed as nurturers, and so it is difficult to picture women in a homicidal role. It is even more difficult to imagine a female killing multiple victims (Holmes & Holmes, 1998).

Fourth, many researchers have mistakenly defined serial murder in general in terms of sexuality. Though deviant sex is a central component of many serial murders, it is not what defines serial murder — nor is it the central component of the crime. According to Egger (1997), sex is not the central feature in serial murder; rather it is the power that the sex represents that is the goal. It is the need for domination that these killers seek.

Take the notorious case of a male serial murderer: Theodore Bundy. Bundy was known for his preoccupation with law enforcement. To be a police officer invokes power over others. This is why many multiple murderers are drawn to the law enforcement field. Similarly, the well-known killers have often been described as being anal-retentive personality types, exerting control over every part of their lives that they could (Cronin, 1996). It is not surprising that these individuals would search for the same power over a helpless victim.

The few studies that have examined females have concentrated on newspaper accounts and court transcripts in order to garner a picture of these offenders and their crimes. What the second-hand data has shown is that female serial killers exhibit a definite pattern of killing. They use less detectable ways to kill than their male counterparts, such as poisons or suffocation instead of knives or guns (Hickey, 1997).

As a result, women do not leave physical marks or evidence when they murder, so they can commit their crimes for longer periods of time without being detected. For instance, the average male serial killer murders on average for 4.2 years before apprehension, but the female averages 8.4 years before she is caught (Hickey, 1997; 1991). Imagine the damage a female can do in those additional four years. This is a frightening statistic but one that will not change until better analysis is conducted.

Without the benefit of personal interviews to integrate into their data, researchers have only been able to hypothesize what thought patterns and background characteristics mold this deviant behavior. Accordingly, the laborious process of conducting painstaking interviews is required, to extract the intimate details of offenders' lives that is lead to crime comprehension. Then, education will be crucial to familiarize law enforcement with this phenomenon. Only then will the timeframe available to females killers start to decrease.

## Profiles

Profiling became popular on television after the movie *The Silence of the Lambs* made it a household term. Creating a personality composite of someone who kills is the job of a profiler, and this can be accomplished because studies have demonstrated specific patterns in crime scenes and established links to specific types of individuals who commit deviant homicides.

Serial killers are typically Causasian males between the ages of 25-35 who prey on powerless Caucasian strangers (Holmes & De Burger, 1988). Obviously, this profile leaves out female offenders. As previously mentioned, no in-depth interviews had been conducted with female offenders due to their small numbers in relation to men and the difficulty of gaining offender cooperation. It has been almost impossible to gain insight into female multiple killers because these females simply do not agree to be interviewed. That is why this research is so important: it is the only study of its kind.

Recently, one researcher had attempted to conduct in-depth interviews with female serial killers (meeting with partial success) prior to this author's work. In 1998, former F.B.I. agent Patricia Kirby, Ph.D., examined gender roles and serial murder by interviewing three female serial killers and five males. Though Dr. Kirby started the project in the hopes of securing the cooperation of more females, it was difficult to obtain permission from them and their attorneys. Kirby found that female serial killers tend to be involved in female-dominated occupations that entail care-giving (Kirby, 1998). And unlike male serial killers who generally use overt methods to kill their victims, female serialists tend to use more subtle ways to murder their victims.

A partial explanation for these covert methods of murder is that the gender role as played by these women tends to be traditional. That is, female serial killers are typically raised in families where there are clear, traditionally defined sex roles within the family unit (Kirby, 1998). Because they come from homes where sex roles are rigorously defined, female serial killers gravitate toward female dominated professions. What this means is that gender role does indeed affect or shape the nature of violence by men and women (Wolfgang, 1958; Ward et al, 1969).

Accordingly, studies have demonstrated that female serial killers tend to gravitate toward jobs that revolve around caring for the infirm As they have most often been raised in homes where they have witnessed females in the role of caretaker, this role provides a sense of comfort and familiarity. Being a caregiver is something they know they can do, and for these offenders who crave the excitement of killing, there is a side benefit to choosing a profession that places them in situations where they are in contact with helpless individuals. Due to the vulnerability of patients or children, it is easier for the female serialist to asphyxiate or poison the victim (Kelleher, 1998). The sick or infirm cannot resist. Plus, when a sick victim dies and there are no overt signs of struggle, it is easy for police and coroners to mistake the crime for a natural death (Cluff et al., 1997). Over 50% of their victims are very old or very young (Hickey, 1997). In essence, the gender role of being in a "feminine" care-giving profession allows the female serial killer easy access to victims.

Male serial killers, on the other hand, tend to be found in jobs that are considered to be more masculine. They often work with their hands in jobs that require strength and stamina, such as construction. Upon examining the backgrounds of males, it was discovered that they tended to come from homes where a female was a domineering caregiver. However, just as for female serial killers, there was strict gender role enforcement in the homes. So, when males emerge from this environment and proceed to select victims, they chose the helpless, just like their female counterparts (Hickey, 1997). Prostitutes and young women tend to be favorite targets since they typically make easy prey. Yet unlike females, males patrol outdoors surroundings, often in a vehicle, instead of choosing someone immediately surrounding them. This reduces the likelihood of being apprehended. Furthermore, males often sexually assault their victims, so the crime can be considered, at least in their minds, a masculine-type homicide. It becomes easy to see how gender role influences male and female killers, and knowing this, law enforcement has an increased opportunity to recognize the crimes when they occur.

Criminologists have also found that beyond using covert methods to kill their victims in a "feminine" way, female serial killers are geographically stable. That means that females do not tend to move from one location to another when they kill, as do many male serial killers. Female predators remain in one locality and cloak their crimes by choosing very sick or very helpless victims. To aid in their crimes, women do not mutilate or torture their victims. Instead, they use poison or asphyxiation to kill. This means that there are no marks or other types of evidence for law enforcement to examine, making detection quite difficult. The pattern appears to be: many deaths surrounding one lone female caregiver.

Again, because no interviews had been conducted with females, criminologists have been left to speculate as to crime motivation. Almost always, the motivation for killing had been attributed to monetary gain (Keeney & Heide, 1994). Often, the female benefits financially as a result of the crimes; however, it would be simplistic to cite money as the main reason why female serial killers act.

As this book will show, financial gain was not the main reason that female serialists chose to become executioners. A far more insidious psychological inspiration emerged during the process of questioning these women.

There is one disconcerting commonality that rears its head upon examining female serialists. There is a tendency for these crimes to occur in the southern United States. In their examination of 14 female serial killers, using secondary data sources, Kenney and Heide (1994) found that half of all noted female serialists killed in southern states. This contrasts with male serial killers, who have most often killed in the Pacific Northwest (Hickey, 1991). There has been no exploratory analysis as to why this should be the case; it is to be hoped that researchers will concentrate on this question in future projects.

Another eerie similarity among female serial killers is the strong connection with their victims. In other words, females predate on those whom they know (Fox & Levin, 1994): a nurse who cares for you in the hospital; your favorite babysitter; even your wife. Female serial killers act like chameleons who blend in with their intended victims and seem to be the last person anyone would suspect. Often they are seen as the *angel of death* in cases where the killer is charged with the care of elderly, infirm, or very young victims who cannot defend themselves. For instance, of all female serial killers between 1826-1995, over 70% killed someone they knew while only 24% killed strangers (Hickey, 1997). This makes victim access so much easier as we all let our guard down when we are with those we know. Again, what better way to kill?

## Mass Murderers — Male vs. Female

Though little known is about female serial killers, we know even less about the female mass murderer. Mass murder in general is much easier to identify and quantify because typically it occurs in one place, and often the perpetrator either commits suicide at the scene or is taken into custody.

Mass murder has been defined as an offense in which "multiple victims are intentionally killed in a single incident" (Palermo, 1997: 1), or as an offense during which several people are killed "at the same time and place, in a single episode of violence," (Lester, 1995: 14). Levin and Fox (1985) define mass killers as killers who kill in one episode at the same time, and Petee et al. (1997: 322) offer an almost identical definition: those who kill at least "three people in a public place." And finally, Dietz (1986: 480) requires that there must be a "willful injury" to five persons, of whom at least three die. For this research, mass murder was defined as the killing of five or more victims in one instance.

Unlike the elusive serial killer, the mass killer is one who seems to explode and kill in public places. The main characteristic appears to be a lack of an emotional cooling-off period between the homicides. The key point is that the killer does not cool down and reflect upon the crime before taking another life. Each homicide is part of one elaborate mental plan.

This can be confusing to those who are unfamiliar with these crimes, because mass murder can occur over a long period of time and at different geographic locations. Charles Whitman illustrates this point. In 1966, Whitman shot 46 people, killing 16 in Austin, Texas. The day prior to the shooting, Whitman had killed his mother in her home and then proceeded to his own home, where he killed his wife. It was the following day that he climbed to the top of the tower at the University of Texas and opened fire on everyone on the ground below (Holmes & Holmes, 1994). Obviously, Mr. Whitman did not "cool off" between the homicides. This was one homicidal episode, although it was spread over more than one day and more than one location.

The profile of the typical mass killer is a white male, over age 25, who has no significant criminal history, and who is perceived as a caring family man or friend (Kelleher, 1997). Existing research indicates that mass murderers live in a world of social deprivation and depression due to an overwhelming lack of coping mechanisms.

Usually, such killers are portrayed as insane — people who finally snapped, with no prior indicators. However, it has been documented that these individuals have suffered incremental stresses all of their lives (Petee et al., 1997). The crux of the phenomenon appears to be dismal coping skills. Simply, mass murderers do not cope well with stresses, especially those that accumulate: daily stress. When the mass murderer has exhausted the ability to remain isolated, the killer makes a lethal decision to "get even" or settle some type of score through violent means (Kelleher, 1997). Being unable to function well in society, the mass killer strikes out because of the misguided belief that others are attempting to sabotage his life. At the juncture where paranoia meets unmanageable stress, an explosion of anger occurs, and lives are lost.

No one knew whether this precarious mindset applied to females, as the available statistical sample was so small in number. From 1929 to 1996, there have been 86 cases of mass murder, ten of which were committed by female offenders between 1977 and 1997 (author's files). Such a rarity had not been considered worthy of study, so — like female serial killers — female mass murderers were largely disregarded in research.

However, when you consider the number of victims killed by each female, it becomes blatantly obvious that women are as lethal as males. Their victim count is high, by any standard. For instance, in 1985, Sylvia Seegrist entered a Springfield Mall in Pennsylvania armed with a .22 caliber semiautomatic rifle and proceeded to shoot ten people. Three people were killed while seven survived (Kelleher, 1997). In 1978, Priscilla Ford drove her Lincoln Continental down a Nevada street and killed several people by running them over. In 1988, LaFonda Fay Foster shot and killed five men and women when she decided that she was fed up with her life. These killers are out there; they simply strike less frequently than men. And when they do kill, they take as many victims as males do, and startlingly, in each of the aforementioned cases, the victims were random. There was no pattern as to whom the women decided to kill. Thus, it appears that female mass murderers can strike at any time and kill any one of us who happens to be their paths. Certainly this is worth at least some study.

### Trends

One interesting characteristic of multiple murders that must be dealt with is the decreasing age of the killer. In 1997, a 14-year-old boy in Paducah, Kentucky killed three classmates and wounded five others in an act of mass murder at Heath High School. This young boy had foreshadowed the incident by telling classmates one week prior that "something big" would happen on Monday (Cichetti, 1997:1). On April 20, 1999, high school students Eric Harris and Dylan Kelbold made their way into Columbine High School in Littleton, Colorado and killed twelve students and one teacher. Harris and Kelbold had created an elaborate plan in which they set off bombs, thus creating a distraction, while they roamed the hallways and shot students (*Cincinnati Enquirer*, 1999). In Dayton, Ohio, an 11-year-old female is the lead suspect in the serial murders of 4 children.

As the profiler on the Dayton case, this author has found it most difficult dealing with the disbelief associated with children committing these crimes. Not only do law enforcement officials have difficulty in accepting that children may be killers, but the general public does not want to believe that a child could be capable of serial or mass murder. Yet, every year we discover younger and younger offenders, and we as a society have little choice but to address the issue — otherwise, innocent people will die for no reason.

Whether male or female, young or old, the ranks of multiple murderers are ever increasing. This phenomenon has an impact on every social stratum — the rich, the poor, the young, the old. Anyone can be targeted by these most insidious predators, who take care to hide their innermost thoughts and deviancies. We have not yet mastered or even created all of the tools that can effectively fight these killers. There will be others tomorrow and next week. How long will we wait before we truly come to understand the most dangerous of human poachers?

## 2.

For as long as people have been studying murder, they have been asking whether nature or nurture creates killers. That is, there is an age-old debate over whether killers are born bad or whether their environment makes them that way. Now, criminologists have created motivational models that attempt to identify why murderers act out. Most of these theories have been individualistic; they include the biogenic, psychological, and social learning models.

### Biological Theories

The biogenic model proposed a biological theory, or physical analysis, in which physical characteristics determined whether one would be a criminal. For example, in the early 1900's, scientists examined physical traits and suggested that specific body structures pointed to criminality. Specifically, they hypothesized that measurements of foreheads, earlobes and the distance between an individual's eyes ultimately determined an individual's proneness to criminality (Lombroso,

1911). Apparently, the popular notion suggested that physical features alone could predict criminality — individuals with such "deformities" as long foreheads or oversized nostrils were considered dangerous, criminals in the making, although no formal studies had confirmed such an idea.

Based on these early suggestive hypotheses, a considerable amount of study concentrated on body style or shape. After facial features came the belief that general body shape could indicate one's criminal predisposition. The theory was that an individual's temperament dictated body type and body type dictated criminal potential. More docile individuals were less likely to exercise and build muscles, and these docile (and less muscular) individuals were considered to be less likely to engage in crime. To test the theory, Sheldon (1940) examined body styles and divided human body shapes into three categories: the endomorph (short and fat), the ectomorph (tall and thin), and the mesomorph (athletic). According to Sheldon, the mesomorph was most likely to have a criminal predisposition. Studies confirmed these findings.

Facial deformity was considered to be related to crime, as well. Interestingly, a link has indeed been established between boys who suffer from severe acne and criminal behavior. On the other hand, boys with no complexion problems were less likely to act against societal norms (Hooton, 1939). The findings were clear, yet there was no explanation as to why acne sufferers were more predisposed to crime than others.

However, it has been shown that social isolation is connected with aggression and criminality, so it can be speculated that because of their severe acne, these individuals may have been outcasts who avoided social interaction (Ressler, et al., 1988); excessive acne may lead to social isolation that in turn can convert into anger. And ultimately, if unchecked, anger leads to violence.

**Biological Theories and Women**

*1. Appearance*

Early scientists applied this biological theory to women and de-cided on certain explanations that later on were been deemed "ideology masquerading as science" (Leyton, 1986: 264). Females were equated with children, beings with small brains. And when it came to criminal-ity, specific physical characteristics were considered predictive. Female criminals supposedly suffered from cranial depressions, deep frontal sinuses, and a heavy lower jaw. In essence, a criminal woman was de-scribed as having masculine facial features. But the most ridiculous proposition was the supposed connection between women's criminal-ity and wrinkles. Early scientists suggested that there was a greater incidence of fronto-vertical wrinkles and crows feet on the faces of criminal women. No research or scientific measurement documented any such link, yet even folklore entered into this theory. It was said that wrinkled, criminal women were similar to witches of lore (Lomboros, 1911). Obviously, such ideas cannot be accepted as predictive of violent behavior; so other physical factors were analyzed.

*2. Genetics*

Instead of merely looking at individuals in order to guess whether a person was destined to commit violent acts, criminologists eventually began examining genetic structure and its possible link to crime. Genes are heredity, and that includes temperament and proclivities. In other words, some authors studying genetic information and its relationship to crime suggest that certain people are born to be violent; they are *born bad*.

Interestingly, it was discovered that many violent offenders had an extra Y chromosome (male chromosome) in their genetic makeup (Cameron & Frazer, 1987). This extra male chromosome was believed to create higher levels of aggression, and since aggression is linked to violent behavior, the extra component was viewed as predictive. However, this theory has not been substantiated.

In fact, it has been refuted. When two groups of violent offenders were compared, it was discovered that those who lacked the extra Y chromosome committed more offenses than those who inherited the extra Y chromosome (Own, 1972). These conflicting results have left scientists in a quandary, and as of yet, no definitive answer has been found.

Using another biological theory, hormones were examined as potential contributors to violence. The theory suggested that offenders act out because their hormones force them to commit crimes. In other words, offenders purportedly have no control over their behavior due to the many hormones (particularly testosterone) raging through their bodies. Indeed, elevated levels of testosterone have been linked to aggression, but the "popular belief that rape and other sexual violence results from uncontrollable urges which themselves are caused by excess androgen is not supported by logic or evidence" (Cameron & Frazer, 1987: 80). One specific verifiable fact is irrefutable: violence, especially sexual assault and sex murder, almost always occurs in private. Serial killers typically do not drag their victims away from a crowded street and kill them with witnesses and police watching their actions. Further, they do not kill every day. Instead, these killers stalk in silence, keeping themselves hidden in order to protect their identities (Hagerty, 1997). Thus it can be argued that if killers truly were ruled by hormones, they would act out whenever their hormones forced them to, not simply when it is advantageous for them to strike. Because many killers stalk and abduct their victims, carefully planning their crimes, it is highly likely that they can control themselves. The likelihood is that they choose their actions. Hormones may simply act as trigger mechanisms, but nothing more.

**Brain Dysfunction**

Yet another biological component considered as potentially contributing to violence is brain dysfunction. Traumatic cranial injuries have been used to explain violent behavior. Many serial killers suffered head trauma in childhood (Cronin, 1996). Thus criminologists have suggested that the brains of such offenders must be damaged from these injuries, and perhaps, the injuries themselves could explain why serial murderers kill. The theory proceeds that when the limbic part of the brain — which provides emotion, anger, and fear — is damaged, it can produce excessive violence (Wilson, 1996; Norris,1988).

Further, serial killers are motivated by internal cognitive functioning in the form of deviant fantasies. A fantasy is an elaborate set of cognitions originating in daydreams and gratifying an unfulfilled desire (Burgess et al., 1994). Fantasies originate in the left hemisphere of the brain, and when a head trauma occurs, "pathologic neural organization for the dominant hemisphere provides the substrate for the abnormal ideational representations of sexual deviations" (Flor-Henry, 1980: 260). In plain language, because fantasy originates in the left hemisphere of the brain, when this area is damaged, then fantasies can become "bizarre" or "deviant" (Gosselin & Wilson, 1984: 95). Bizarre fantasies are central to serial killers. They rely upon their elaborate daydreams when they plan their crimes (Cronin, 1996). And so it may make sense to conjecture that a head injury, which leads to deviant fantasies, can lead to multiple murder. There is not enough research to verify that brain damage specifically causes serial crimes, but it is worth mentioning and should be studied further.

Likewise, brain-wave abnormalities are purported to explain the phenomenon of serial murder (Norris, 1988). One half of the psychopathic population suffers from brain-wave abnormalities, but only fifteen percent of the non-psychopathic population suffers from this defect (Mawson & Mawson, 1977). As a majority of experts agree that most serial killers are psychopaths, it has been suggested that brain-wave abnormalities could cause serial murder (Norris, 1988); that in an individual who is both psychopathic and has brain-wave dysfunction, there is a greater likelihood that violent behavior will result. However, though half of all psychopaths endure brain-wave abnormalities, it cannot be said that that percentage of the psychopathic population engages in serial murder. Though the potential for contribution is high, brainwave functioning alone is an insufficient causal factor.

In summary, many researchers have attempted to find a single biological component that explains or causes serial homicide. Many biological aspects, including hormones, extra chromosomes, brain dysfunction, and specific physical traits have been explored as possible contributing factors. Yet, no direct or consistent correlations have been found. Therefore, scientists have been forced to take a more holistic approach to examining the causes of serial murder. Biology is only one variable. Other factors such as social stratum and psychological inputs are likely to affect an individual's behavior as well.

## Psychology

Psychology has attempted to create interpretations for the concepts of multiple murder by defining serial killers and mass murderers as psychopaths, by labeling them as insane, implicating depression, and by examining family background. These potential factors indicate an emotional component as a cause of violent behavior, ignoring the biological and sociological propositions. Psychological explanations are basic theoretical concepts that must be addressed when studying the phenomenon of multiple murder.

### Psychopath

Psychopathology has been characterized as a disturbance which is defined by aggression and a lack of personal attachments or the ability to bond with another human being (Meloy, 1988). Psychopaths are "completely lacking in conscience and in feelings for others, they selfishly take what they want and do as they please, violating social norms and expectations without the slightest sense of guilt or regret" (Hare, 1993: 5). For these reasons, researchers have referred to psychopaths as "affectionless characters" (Bowlby, 1944). Similarly, Cleckley (1981) simplified psychopathic traits into sixteen features including lack of remorse for harmful acts, failure to learn by punishment, and the presentation of a charming veneer. Those affected by the disorder also showed chronic lying, defiance, persistent aggression, early experimentation with sex, cruelty to animals and other children, and a predisposition for setting fires.

What is remarkable about the disorder is that psychopaths feel no shame for their misdeeds (Cleckley, 1981). Individuals who are psychopathic tend to lack remorse for harmful acts (Reich, 1945). In fact, when Reich (1945) examined a group of psychopaths, he found that they evinced little reaction to the results of their aggressive behaviors. Cleckley (1981) and Meloy (1988) found a remarkable lack of empathy in young psychopaths, a void so great as to impact behavior. It has been hypothesized that psychopaths lack a capacity to bond or form attachments (creating empathy) because they failed to receive consistent and sensitive caring when young (Bowlby, 1979). When examining multiple murderers, a marked lack of empathy for the suffering of others is prominent.

In order to better understand psychopathy and how it relates to multiple murder, one must comprehend what a psychopath is. There are different types of psychopaths, just as there are diverse kinds of people. Hare (1993) suggested that psychopaths can be divided into three broad categories which cover the spectrum of the disorder. These categories are the primary, secondary and dyssocial psychopaths.

The primary psychopath is one who has no fear or anxiety. This is an individual who enjoys being stimulated, no matter the cost to himself or others. A primary psychopath attempts to create a sense of imbalance or excitement through his actions. This person tends to show very poor judgment and is overly impulsive. The goal is self-stimulation.

The secondary psychopath has emotional problems and does feel guilt upon acting out. The key difference between the primary and secondary psychopath is the stress level endured during the course of offending. The secondary psychopath engages in repeated criminal behavior and suffers from intense anxiety. The line between primary and secondary psychopath is thin, yet the primary psychopath feels no stress while the secondary psychopath is acutely stressed. However, whether there is a sense of anxiety or not does not appear to impact the psychopath's decision to engage in deviant behavior.

Finally, the dyssocial psychopath acts within the norm of his delinquent group, while acting in a way that is detrimental to society. That is, the dyssocial psychopath will commit criminal acts as long as they do not conflict with a group of friends or cohorts. For instance, a gang member shows loyalty to the gang and engages in socially unacceptable behavior that is sanctioned within the peer group (Hare, 1993). However, the dyssocial psychopath most often will not victimize members of the gang, because to do so would be viewed as wrong. Thus, the dyssocial psychopath recognizes the difference between right and wrong, but the inhibition against acting out only applies to doing so within the group. It is alright to victimize an outsider, but victimizing a gang member is off limits.

## Serial Murder and Psychopaths

It has been noted that the psychopath is not like the normal person (Meloy, 1988). Feelings of omnipotence dominate a psychopath's mind (Horney, 1945). The psychopath sees the self as superior to others, so in that individual's mind, he or she is smarter, faster, and better than everyone else (Geberth, 1998). Because the psychopath holds a narcissistic self-concept (viewing the self as superior), the psychopath has low regard for other people. This inflated self-view aids in explaining why the psychopath lies, cheats, and acts aggressively. It has been suggested that these aggressive psychopathic behaviors are caused by a desire for constant stimulation (as in the primary psychopath). McCord and McCord (1956) found that psychopaths continually crave excitement, and their deviant behaviors of lying, manipulating, and acting out stem from this obsessive desire to be stimulated or entertained.

When the psychopath successfully manipulates people, there is a feeling of excitement and exhilaration much like a runner would feel when victorious in a race (Bursten, 1973a). The successful manipulation or "win" is proof to the psychopath that he or she is a superior human being. With such an attitude, it is intolerable for the psychopath to fail or be placed in a submissive position. A "loss" or failure to achieve a goal threatens the self-perception of omnipotence; but instead of recognizing individual deficits and shortcomings, the psychopath denies the failure (Rothstein, 1980). Though the psychopath denies the failure to the outside world, the failure serves to increase the narcissistic-like persona and to veil inner feelings of low self worth.

Instead of accepting limitations, the psychopath denies them; the denial, however, is external. Over time, incremental stresses become overwhelming for the psychopath who cannot function when his or her behavior or judgment is questioned. What might seem trivial to most people will be taken as lifelong insult to a psychopathic individual (Geberth, 1998; Meloy, 1988). The psychopath harbors the anger that is brought about by an insult or slight, and ultimately, this unchecked anger feeds a fire of revenge either against the individual who angered the psychopath or someone in a vulnerable position (Meloy, 1988). The psychopath literally cannot process an insult and move forward. This individual must restore his grandiose mental picture of himself, and the only way the psychopath has learned to do so is to act deviantly, whether by lying, cheating, or even killing.

The inability to process failure or stress affects the psychopath in a very unusual way. Coping strategies are employed, but those used are not healthy and only serve to create higher levels of anger and frustration. Because the psychopath cannot accept that he or she has faults or may have been at fault in a situation, bad traits are transferred onto a vulnerable victim (Meloy, 1988). This is called projection. Simply, potential victims are seen as lesser beings who deserve to be harmed. That way, it becomes quite easy to harm an innocent victim. When the psychopath endures a failure, instead of acknowledging fault, he or she projects the painful inner feelings onto a vulnerable victim. Victims are compartmentalized into stereotypes in order to minimize what he or she intends to do (Hagerty, 1997).

Applied directly to the serial killer, this concept is clear. Serial killers cannot accept criticism or stress, and when such circumstances arise, the psychopathic killer engages in projection. In addition, the psychopathic serial killer engages in objectification (Cronin, 1996). Objectification is the process of viewing others as a thing instead of a person.

The serial killer does, indeed, view potential victims as objects instead of human beings. Interviews with male serial killers have elucidated this process. If the killer stalks a woman, the killer views her as a whore instead of a wife or mother. Likewise, if a pedophile abducts a child, the child is viewed as a runaway and deserving of harm. Killing the elderly or the sick is justified by saying that those victims would die soon anyway. Such objectification allows the psychopathic killer to do what he or she intends to do without feeling a hint of remorse (Holmes, 1996).

When the psychopathic killer is under duress, he or she is likely to project undesirable traits onto vulnerable victims and to view the victim as an object. Once projection and objectification occur, the killer can strike out violently with no feelings or remorse. Simply, the killer can commit heinous acts because in the mindset of a serial killer, the victim is a bad person who deserves whatever pain is inflicted. Stress has built to a point where the grandiose image has been questioned, projection and objectification occur, and violence then is almost a certainty. This is how the multiple murderer operates.

In summary, both serial and mass murderers appear to suffer from emotional dysfunction and they live with high levels of anxiety. Though they are anxious, they do not feel remorse for their actions. The high anxiety levels emerge from an inability to effectively handle life's stressors. Holding down a job and dealing with being subordinate in a workplace situation are extremely difficult for the multiple killer, as these roles conflict with the grandiose self-view. Reality paints a different picture (of an inadequate self) which results in anger and frustration (Kelleher, 1997). After this anxiety builds to an unbearable point, the serial killer and mass murderer typically release the stress by committing the act of homicide (Cronin, 1996). This could help explain why the serial killer engages in repeated homicides: to alleviate stress while at the same time self-stimulating. Documented evidence shows that multiple murderers have reported feelings of calm and peace after committing their crimes (Hagerty, 1997; Holmes, 1996).

However, tempting as it may be to label multiple murderers as psychopaths, that does not provide an answer as to why these people repeatedly kill. It cannot simply be said that psychopathy explains multiple murder because not all psychopaths become serial killers or mass murderers (Holmes & Holmes, 1994). There are psychopaths who do function in society without becoming violent.

Speculation exists that psychopaths who do not become violent concentrate their work into indirectly violent situations such as jobs that require working with instruments. In those cases, instruments such as hammers, knives (surgeons), or even guns (police officers) are used. This allows the individual to feel powerful and in some instances to act violently, which alleviates high stress levels.

**Mental Illness**

Psychiatric illnesses have been linked to violence, so it is not surprising that multiple personality disorder and psychosis both have been considered as possible motivating factors for multicide. Multiple personality disorder occurs when more than one personality exists within one person. Each personality is unique and, many times, the person is unaware that several personas cohabitate within the body. As it applies to serial murder, it has been suggested that a "bad" personality acts out, and the "good" personality is unaware of the killings.

For example, from October 1977 to January 1979, Kenneth Bianchi and his cousin Angelo Buono together strangled 10 women in the Los Angeles area. The pair became known as the "Hillside Strangler," because after torturing and killing their victims, they dumped the victims' bodies on hillsides (Lane & Gregg, 1995). During his trial, Bianchi tried to convince the court that he suffered from multiple personality disorder. He claimed that it was his alter ego "Steve" who committed the crimes and that he was unaware of "Steve's" activities (Lane & Gregg, 1995). During close examination, it was determined that Bianchi was faking the disorder in an attempt to receive a lenient sentence. In fact, no well-documented case of serial murder has ever been explained by a diagnosis of multiple personality disorder (Hickey, 1991). Therefore, theorists have had to look elsewhere for links between mental illness and multiple murder.

There has even been speculation that serial killers have suffered a psychotic break with reality. A psychosis entails a disconnection from internal and external reality. In other words, a psychotic individual will have difficulty interpreting events from the outside world as well as events in his or her own mind. This leads to confusion; the psychotic individual is confuses delusions with reality. More specifically, a psychotic individual will suffer from a break between feeling, thinking, and acting (Jackson & Bekerian, 1997). A psychotic individual has trouble identifying reality, and this often leads to hallucinations (seeing visions or hearing voices) and delusions (strongly held but misguided beliefs).

While it would be tempting to suggest that multiple killers must be psychotic, it would be very difficult for such an individual to execute several murders without being caught. Therefore, there are few serial killers who are truly psychotic (Egger, 1997). In fact, most serial killers are not psychotic (Geberth, 1997; Hickey, 1991; Leyton, 1986).

As is often pointed out, serial killers are methodical in their killings. They do not kill in front of witnesses. They take their victims when no one is watching, and they bring the victims to even more secluded places in order to execute their crimes. It would follow that if serial killers were psychotic and were striking out in response to voices or hallucinations, then there would be little or no attempt at all to hide their identity due to the high level of mental disorganization. However, it is well known that most male serial killers take great pains to ensure that no one discovers who they are, so that they can continue to kill undetected (Cronin, 1996).

On the other hand, many documented cases of mass murder have demonstrated some element of psychosis. That is, many mass murderers suffer from a break with reality, and this is said to lead to their crimes. It is difficult to explain acts of mass violence in any other way, so insanity is a convenient label to apply to such offenders (Kelleher, 1997). Several mass murderers have been shown to suffer from paranoia and paranoid schizophrenia (Kelleher, 1997). Mass murderers are often obsessively paranoid, to the point of blaming others in society for their personal shortcomings (Palermo, 1997). It has been said that mass murderers "may be suffering from a borderline personality disturbance, depression or paranoia with explosive outbursts of destructive aggression," (Kelleher, 1997: 66).

Priscilla Ford would constitute a mass murderer who suffered from a mental illness. In November 1980, when Ford drove her Buick automobile down a Reno, Nevada, sidewalk killing six people, she did it in response to voices which told her to kill (Holmes & Holmes, 1994). Clearly, Ford was suffering from some form of mental illness. Thus, there appears to be a connection between psychosis and mass murder, but there is insufficient data to pinpoint how many mass kill-ers suffer from the disorder.

The general public has endeavored to label such crimes as the acts of insane individuals, yet when examining the motivational models in-volved in multicide, the majority of cases do not support this theory. In fact, insanity only appears in a fraction of documented cases (Kelleher, 1997; Levin & Fox, 1985). From these few instances, there has been an unreliable extrapolation to the entire population of mass murderers, at least in popular media.

In reality, the facts demonstrate a much more sinister component. It is more typical for a mass murderer to plan the offense and to be lucid when doing so, than to kill in response to delusions or hallucinations (Kelleher, 1997; Levin & Fox, 1985, 1991; Palermo, 1997).

25-year-old Sylvia Seegrist was known to dress in military attire and to stalk people. At around 3:30 p.m on October 30, 1985, she walked into the Springfield Mall in Delaware County, Pennsylvania, and fired a .22-caliber semiautomatic weapon (Kelleher, 1997). Seegrist began shooting at people, including children. Three people were killed, including a two-year-old child. When asked why she did it, Seegrist replied, "my family makes me nervous." (Kelleher, 1997: 134). This mass murderer had a history of mental illness, yet she was able to get and use a gun within a public facility. She did not simply shoot people on her way to the mall; she waited until she reached the mall before she opened fire.

In summary, it would be overly simplistic to attribute multicidal motivations to insanity alone. Though a factor in some mass killings, insanity has only been documented in very few rare instances. Most serial killers do not suffer from a break with reality, and they are not psychotic. They do suffer from personality disorders such as psychopa-thology, which aids in explaining why they can commit outrageous crimes with little to no feelings of remorse. It must be noted that some mass murderers suffer from a psychosis, which alters their perceptions of reality. Yet, clearly, few bear such a mental impairment. In most cases, mental disorganization does not interfere with planning and execution of these vicious crimes. Therefore, like psychopathology, mental illness alone can neither explain nor mitigate the acts of serial and mass murderers. It can be a contributing factor, but in and of itself, it is an insufficient explanation at best.

### Over-controlled versus Under-controlled

As criminologists struggled to find explanations and causes for multicide, psychologists and psychiatrists examined how diseases and disorders of the mind are connected with serial and mass murder. Research began to take a typological approach, looking beyond the psychopath or the insane individual to categories of people most closely associated with such killings.

After careful analysis, two personality typologies were found to closely match individuals who engage in one-time homicides. These one-time killers were divided into three groups. Each group was unique and clearly delineated:

- Over-controlled personality
- Under-controlled personality
- Subcategories

The over-controlled person is inhibited against committing violent acts, almost to the point of being obsessive. Anger is held inside instead of being released when the individual is threatened or challenged. Brooding is this individual's coping mechanism, and holding on to past insults and anger is common. It is when the over-controlled personality has endured years of frustration that a boiling point is reached. After repeated exposure to stress and frustration, the over-controlled personality eventually strikes out with violence. What is remarkable about this type of killer is the severity of violence that is inflicted on a victim. Typically, damage will be extreme in nature, often appearing as if it has taken place in a frenzy. There are multiple victim wounds and a bloody crime scene, which reveals a person who has exploded.

One might suggest that the over-controlled personality is the example of a mass killer who strikes out at large numbers of individuals with extreme forms of violence after brooding and harboring insults for long periods of time. The mass murderer internalizes anger and typically has little to no violent history. Likewise, it has been speculated that serial killers suffer from a myriad of troubles that lead to high stress levels and inability to cope. The repeated homicides may act as an outlet for the frustration and anger caused by stress. In many instances, the serial killer is not violent in other aspects of life — the homicides are the only outbursts; so the over-controlled personality type might be applicable to this offender as well.

In contrast, the under-controlled personality has no moral difficulty with aggression and violence. This is the type of person who will react with violence before thinking, and actually prefers to act out. There is often little or no provocation to violence, and the outbursts tend to be short-lived and frequent. An under-controlled personality uses violence to get his or her own way, and those who know such people would categorize them as explosive. Aggression is viewed as a means to an end, and is used in daily life. Such people are constantly starting fights with neighbors, on the road, or in bars. Overall, this is not the portrait of a mass murderer or a serial killer; such killers are subtler in their actions (at least while they are not killing).

Because some offenders have appeared to fall in between these categories, criminologists broke the over-controlled and under-controlled personalities into four subcategories. It is here that a much more direct application emerges for serial and mass murderers. Blackburn (1969) developed four groups:

- Over-controlled-repressor
- Depressed-inhibited
- Paranoid-aggressive
- Psychopathic

First, the hallmark of the *over-controlled-repressor* killer is denial. Denial is used as a coping mechanism for stress reduction. Likewise, a high degree of impulse control is exhibited. Coupled with the denial and self restraint is a marked sense of anxiety and uneasiness; this type of killer is very edgy. Jumpy. High-strung. Essentially, the over-controlled repressor is likely to suppress anger and then explode in one episode of violence (Blackburn, 1969). When this occurs, the offender feels intense stress that builds, even after the crime has taken place.

The second sub-category is the *depressed-inhibited*. Typically, they are schizophrenic (psychotic) individuals who have mental breaks with reality. At the same time, they exhibit a high level of impulse control throughout their daily lives and are careful not to upset the status quo. Depression is prominent, and interpersonal contact is restricted. When depressed-inhibited killers act out, they murder in one severe act that is likely to resemble a gruesome massacre. The crime scenes will be bloody because such killers are out of touch with reality and often are killing as a result of a hallucination or delusion. There is overkill and victim obliteration.

The *paranoid-aggressive* group was labeled the "most disturbed" by

Blackburn (1969: 17) because such individuals are introverts who are impulsive and prone to violence. They suffer a plethora of psychological difficulties including depression and hypochondriosis. Essentially, they are easily disturbed and quick to act with violence when threatened. Unlike the view of over-controlled characters, being docile (repressed) is viewed as being weak, and such a label is not an option in this person's mindset. Because there is a tendency to fly off the handle and react with violence to seemingly slight provocation, there is often a lengthy police record in this person's background. The best description would be a hot-head known for having a hot temper.

But it is the fourth category, the *psychopath*, which comes close to resembling the serial killer. Blackburn's psychopath (1969) is quick to anger and to display hostility, and impulsiveness, with little sense of social anxiety. When angered to the point of humiliation, they use violence to achieve their goals. Hurting is seen as instrumental to achieving satisfaction. That is, manipulating and inflicting harm is a means to an end of feeling better, superior. In other words, the psychopath has little inhibition against the use of violence in order to make the self feel better (Blackburn, 1969).

The mass murderer resembles the over-controlled personality in that usually he or she does not engage in violent behavior prior to the acts of mass violence. In any cases, the mass murderer has no arrest history prior to the act of multiple murder. Rage and depression build to the point of an emotional explosion, whereupon the process of killing becomes almost inevitable.

Certainly, such classifications aid in understanding who the serial killers and mass murderers are, but the use for explanatory research is limited. Again, finding one lone explanation appears impossible. Thus, further reflection regarding the minds of multiple murderers must be conducted.

**Depression**

Depression has been said to be linked with sexual murder and sexual aggression in that it serves to fan the fire of rage and hopelessness that is buried within the serial predator. Anger comes from pain, and depression comes from rage. It is proposed that as the despair and anger grow within multiple murderers, inhibitions begin to break down, leading to the violent episode (Revitch & Schlessinger, 1989). So it would appear as if there could be some connection between depression and multicide.

And yet, when sexual murder turns to serial homicide, the killer is often said to be a psychopath who, in turn, cannot endure the range of human emotions and cannot suffer from depression (Meloy, 1988). It has been found that the true psychopath is incapable of feeling the emotions necessary to suffer from depression. For the psychopath's self-concept is incredibly grandiose, and with this sense of grandeur there is none of that discrepancy between actual and ideal self-representations that creates the feeling of worthlessness. On the other hand, the psychopath can become angry at perceived injustices and react accordingly. Thus, anger becomes the best approximation of depression that the psychopath can experience (Yochelson & Samenow, 1977).

When it comes to mass murder, however, researchers have discovered that these offenders often suffer from bouts of depression (Kelleher, 1997). In fact, depression and paranoia are strongly linked with mass murderers (Palermo, 1997). Rejection has occurred in the lives of those who offend in this way. Whether having been fired, divorced, or having lost a loved one, the mass killer is distraught when acting out.

Take the example of 34-year-old Alan Eugene Miller who was arrested in Billingsley, Alabama after he allegedly shot and killed 3 people at his former place of employment. Miller had recently been fired. He was described by his mother as someone who "didn't bother anybody" (Cincinnati Enquirer, 1999: A2). Another example is Mark Barton, who was allegedly responsible for the deaths of 9 people at a brokerage firm in Atlanta, in July, 1999. Barton had recently sustained a substantial loss in the stock market. In a suicide note, he wrote that he had killed his wife first because "she was one of the main reasons for my demise" (Pettys, 1999: A8). Intense paranoia and depression lead to high levels of isolation and extreme sadness for the mass murderer (Kelleher, 1997). The killings result from long periods of isolation, hopelessness, and frustrations. Certainly the connection is clear and is worthy of further analysis.

In summary, although psychological theories provide solid frameworks within which to place these killers, they alone cannot account for repeated homicides. It is consistently pointed out that psychological theories detail little about serial and mass murder (Levin & Fox, 1985). The individual characteristics that are found in serial killers are also found in a large part of the population, which is not homicidal. Furthermore, psychological theories are taken from a small number of unrepresentative cases and extrapolated to all serial killers. What might be causative to one may not necessarily impact another (Levin & Fox, 1985). Similarly, to label someone as suffering from a personality disorder, specifically psychopathology, suggests a medical and/or pathogenic origin, but when examining the serial killer, there are no obvious organic and/or psychotic origins (Canter, 1994).

Much like the biological components, psychological components in and of themselves cannot explain multicide. Psychosis and depression only appear to be factors that are sometimes present when a person kills. Therefore, although psychological states of insanity, depression, and psychopathology have been linked with mass and serial murder, these psychological theories alone cannot attempt to create comprehensive coverage of motivational models.

## Sociology

Because psychology has failed in its attempts to create a comprehensive theoretical foundation for the antecedents of multiple violence, criminologists, sociologists, and researchers from other disciplines have attempted to study multiple murder etiology from other sources. Factors that come from within the criminal are considered in tandem with external influences that may serve to motivate deviant behavior. Theories of labeling, neutralization, and family functioning as a sociological system have been postulated.

## Labeling Theory

In the 1950's, labeling theory suggested that when an individual committed an act of criminality, the individual was committing what was called primary deviance. However when one graduated on to committing several acts of criminality, this was referred to as secondary deviance (Lemert, 1951). In other words, one wrong act is primary, many wrong and gradually worse acts are secondary. The person who entered into secondary deviance was considered, and labeled, more deviant than one who committed a single criminal act. Someone who makes one mistake is more easily forgiven than a repeat offender. As labeling theory submitted, the name or notion applied to an individual was damning. That is, an individual who was labeled "criminal" would, in essence, fulfill the prophecy or the label and become more criminal (Lemert, 1951). The labeling theory predicted that by society, by imprinting someone who committed primary deviance as criminal, served to motivate that individual to commit acts of secondary deviance or criminality (Lemert, 1951). Simply, the labels tarnished the person's self image, and the idea was that if someone calls me "x," then I will be "x."

More modern criminologists have taken the viewpoint that it is absurd to suggest that just because one was called a bank robber that one was destined to be a bank robber. However, labeling was considered substantive. It was the manner in which labels were placed on an individual that appeared to make socialization to the norm more difficult (Becker, 1963). Having a negative label applied by someone perceived (by the individual) as powerful would have a more significant impact than having a label applied by someone of the same or lesser status (Becker, 1963). For instance, it was suggested that being labeled a psychopath by a clinician was far more detrimental to an individual than being labeled a psychopath by a police officer or someone not professional trained, because the clinician's perceived higher social status carried more interpretive weight in an individual's mind.

However, the theory does nothing to elucidate the etiology of multiple murder. One certainly is not labeled a serial killer or a mass murderer from early childhood, when the antecedents of deviant cognitions and behavior begin. The labels are applied much later in life. Thus a label is far from damning to a multiple murderer. Labels can define a person's status as the aging process occurs, but the label simply cannot explain the origins of multiple homicide (Hickey, 1991).

**Neutralization Theory**

No one is bad all of the time. Whether criminal or simple delinquent, everyone at one time or another has acted within societal constraint. Likewise, criminals move in and out of acceptable roles in society. At times, they commit horrific criminal acts, yet at other times, these same individuals drive on the road within the speed limit, eat out at restaurants, and attend social functions. Sykes and Matza (1957) suggest that criminals know what is permissible and what is prohibited, and having this knowledge, they must create cognitive equilibrium with the disparity between right and wrong. Instead of ceasing the deviant behavior, criminals neutralize their actions by changing their self perceptions. They cannot view themselves as predators, so proclaiming themselves victims is a reliable means to neutralize the mental incongruity. In other words, criminals often claim that they have been harmed, and that that entitled them to their wrongdoings.

Criminals tend to view the world in an "us" versus "them" mentality (Sykes & Matza, 1957: 34). Other people act upon them, not the other way around. The mental reorganization that takes place puts the criminal in the role of victim. Not only do they paint themselves as victims, but they minimize the consequences of their actions. It is argued that an act is less wrong because of mitigating circumstances. For example, a criminal may maintain that prostitutes place themselves in risky situations, so it is not so wrong to steal from or rape them. Or perhaps the rich man did not need the money anyway. The wrongdoing is offset by the fact that the victim was not truly harmed, in the eyes of the offender.

Finally, criminals seek fault with contemporary society in order to neutralize the incongruity. They, in essence, condemn the condemners. They view the law as if the law is incorrect, and they seek out examples of faulty applications of the law for self vindication (Sykes & Matza, 1957). They focus on examples of abusive police officers and corrupt politicians, and ask questions like, "if the people who are making the laws are imperfect, how can their laws be effective?". This process occurs continually until the offender reaches a state of mental stability.

Therefore, neutralization theory proposes that criminal offenders minimize the consequences of their crimes because there is no one who is without fault.

This concept is directly applicable to multiple homicides. Neutralization behavior (or in psychology, "projection") is seen when killers objectify and project undesirable traits onto their victims (Hickey, 1997). It is likely that this process is longitudinal for the multiple offender, having its roots in childhood and continuing through adulthood. Such behavior and thoughts help shed light on how killers are able to commit heinous crimes and continue functioning without failure.

### Foundations

Biological, psychological, and sociological theories demonstrate effective categorization and ideas that present interesting analyses of multicide. There are links to genetics, personality disorders, and sociological impacts which cannot be ignored. Yet, any one component cannot create a multiple killer. A mixture of many factors merges to form the mentality necessary to enter into the deviant realm. The multiple murderer is developed over time, and what this research discovered was that when a certain group of events line up in a specific order, there is a greater likelihood of violence than if such events did not unfold. The predictive value of the background factors is limited, but strong correlations suggest that they cannot be ignored.

# 3

## FEMALE MULTIPLE MURDERERS:
## UP CLOSE AND PERSONAL

Who knew? Who could possibly have recognized the dangers? Though if one were to glance closely at what lies behind some caregiver's mask, the teeth of death can be seen quite clearly. Like the jaws of an oversized great white shark, female multiple murderers can be lethal. They devour their prey — for poison is the weapon of choice for female serialists. Those who have managed to survive an attempted murder by these killers have described being poisoned as the equivalent to being eaten alive, much like a shark biting a person in half. This is a horrible visual, yet it is remarkably accurate. And female mass murderers are just as horrid, mowing down pedestrians, cutting victims apart, blasting people to death. Obviously, there is a problem here, and that is why such painstaking steps were taken to interview these most reclusive predators.

Scientists had failed in their attempts to gather a large group of female multiple killers for research interviews, much to the dismay of those who study multicide. Time has demonstrated that getting to the root of an offender's history and thought processes not only can help solve crimes, but also can aid in prevention of these heinous events. Studying the behavioral patterns and mental mechanics involved in multicide has allowed clinicians to better recognize warning signs in young boys. Such important information as the *triad of serial murder* was discovered upon examining the childhoods of boys who grew up to commit multiple murder. The triad includes:

- Firesetting-perpetual activity
- Bedwetting-past age 11
- Cruelty to animals

Clinicians have come to recognize these warning signs and intervene when faced with such behaviors. Additionally, when police build cases against suspects who are linked with multiple homicides, the presence of these background characteristics helps to bolster their cases. The benefits are substantial, and one can plainly see why it is so important to conduct parallel research on females.

When looking at serial and mass murder individually, prior studies demonstrate two striking weaknesses. First, there has been much debate over the definition of serial murder, and questions have arisen as to whether the crime should include sexual deviance. There is no agreement in the criminology field. However, more and more researchers are beginning to recognize that serial murder takes many forms. There are the media-popular lust murderers, who enjoy sexual violence as part of their crimes, but "soft" killers exist as well. These "soft" killers do not torture or rape their victims, yet they do kill in a series in order to create a feeling of power. Because of the confusion over the definition, many serial killers have been ignored and left out of prior research studies. The most notable segment is the female offender.

Another reason for the discrepancy in research analysis is the strict numbers. The phenomenon of female-perpetrated multicide is relatively rare. Terrorist attacks are relatively rare, too; however, no one wishes to be caught in a plane or a building where a terrorist bomb has been planted, and certainly, no one wants to be in the hospital bed with a female serial killer as nurse. Both occurrences are uncommon, but when considered, it becomes apparent that study is essential so that these crimes *remain* rare and can be avoided. We take great pains to provide x-ray machines in airports and metal detectors in federal buildings, all because we fear the rarity known as a terrorist attack. Think of female multicidal offenders in the same vein. At all times it is possible to be a victim. Education is the key to being forearmed.

The purpose of this research was to examine the internal dynamics of female-perpetrated multicide. In order to create a direct link into the mental functioning of these offenders, personal, in-depth interviews were required. However, classifying and predicting individual characteristics and actions involves review of not only primary data sources (offender interviews) but secondary data sources as well. This creates a more objective approach to primary data source response, as offender interviews are subjective in nature. Therefore, secondary data sources included police and autopsy reports, court transcripts, school records, and newspaper accounts to verify information extracted during the interview process. The secondary sources acted as a guideline to which the author can return to when faced with questionable research responses.

It is hypothesized that thought patterns and background factors (childhood) influence the lives and ultimately the crimes committed by women who evolve into multiple murderers. That is, it is suggested that lifestyle and cognitive variables are positively related to repetitive and focused violent behavior. Therefore, a research study focusing on the mental and social functioning (underlying structure) of multiple murderers allows for the most penetrating analysis of these types of offenders. Put simply, a multiple murderer's childhood affects how that individual views the world and therefore how he or she acts in life.

This is a psychosocial approach. Elements of psychology, sociology, forensic science, and criminology are included, since each discipline effects how multiple murderers are created and function. It is proposed that the multiple murderer's underlying familial structure will influence cognitive and behavioral functioning in the forms of thought patterns, play activities, worldview, empathy, and social activities. It is further proposed that the underlying structure acts on a continuum which becomes more focused as the offender becomes more mature. For instance, as a child grows and explores situations outside of the home, it is common for that child to use behaviors exhibited within the home. This is known as modeling. The modeled behavior is ingrained and highly resistant to change. Therefore, when a child interacts with others, he or she is likely to use those behaviors learned within the home, and when that child reaches adulthood, those behaviors are referenced frequently even on an unconscious level. In essence, we use what we know.

**Theory**

As stated above, the particular focus of this study is to describe general characteristics of female multiple murderers by conducting several in-depth interviews with seven female multiple murderers. Specifically, interviews were conducted with women convicted of either serial or mass murder. We will use the Holmes & DeBurger (1985) definition of serial murder: the killing of two or more people over a period of more than 30 days; and the Holmes & Holmes (1994:71) definition of mass murder: the killing of a number of persons in one time and in one place.

Existing records do not contain thought patterns, style of dress, automobile type, fantasy life, attitudes, or personal accounts of home life. Furthermore, official records reveal no in-depth information about what the offender was feeling while she committed her murders. Therefore, this research attempts to describe general characteristics of the female multiple murderer as obtained through one-on-one interviews.

Specifically, the concept of this project was to obtain an insight into offenders' thoughts, feelings, and actions as interpreted through in-depth interviews with the offenders themselves. The idea was that if certain commonalities were detected, perhaps the findings could assist school counselors, criminologists, police officers, and juvenile-delinquency professionals. The Federal Bureau of Investigation conducted similar research in the early 1980's, as mentioned earlier, and their results are widely used and accepted today. Specifically, the F.B.I. interviewed 29 male serial killers from 1979 through 1982. The F.B.I.'s research described "the characteristics of the study population of murderers, the manner in which they committed their crimes, and the crime scenes," (Ressler et al., 1988: 10). The F.B.I. admits that the sample was not random, yet there was a belief that the results could be extrapolated to indicate "general characteristics of sexual murderers" (Ressler et al., 1988).

The results of the research produced an interesting dichotomy that is used in profiling violent crimes. The F.B.I. found that male serial killers tend to fall into an organized or disorganized category (Ressler et al., 1988). The dichotomy is as shown in the table on the next page:

Though the F.B.I.'s research has been valuable to researchers and law enforcement officials, no similar in-depth interviews had been conducted, focusing solely on the female multiple murderer. It had been theorized that the females were driven by greed and lust (Hale & Bolvin, 1998). However, there was no research to document these assertions.

| Organized | Disorganized |
|---|---|
| 1. very intelligent | 1. below average intelligence |
| 2. oldest child | 2. youngest child |
| 3. masculine image | 3. socially immature |
| 4. charismatic | 4. seldom dates |
| 5. socially capable | 5. high school dropout |
| 6. sexually capable | 6. lives alone |
| 7. occupationally mobile | 7. nocturnal |
| 8. lives with partner | 8. lives near crime scene |
| 9. high interest in crime in the news | 9. sloppy appearance |

Amazingly, no one ever bothered to ask the offenders themselves why they killed.

This book attempts to fill this void by approximating the F.B.I.'s analysis of males. Because the number of females who commit mass murder is limited, the author has included three female mass murderers in the current study in order to gain some insight into their cognitive functioning and behaviors. Therefore, this research examines the mindsets of both female serial killers and female mass murderers.

The focus is on what creates and builds these offenders. There are obvious limitations inherent in this research, but it is hoped that the results can be used by police, corrections personnel, and researchers as a baseline of information from which to build additional information and theory.

**Protection of Research Participants**

It is a researcher's ethical obligation to ensure the privacy of all research subjects. The research process must provide for the mental and physical welfare of all participants. Clearly, the women involved in this research are vulnerable, due to incarceration. Accordingly, all the women involved in this research were provided with the assurance of anonymity. Given this assurance, the women agreed to participate, given the likelihood that the results could be helpful to people who have gone through or will go through similar experiences. It is note-worthy that all seven women felt that it was their obligation to partici-pate in order to share their experiences. They viewed granting the in-terview as a means of helping others. Whether this was the true reason can be left for speculation, but in the very least, their participation did allow for the discovery of useful information.

### Research Methodology

Because of the unique nature of the phenomenon, all recognized members of the population of candidates (26 total) were identified through exhaustive research of professional literature, newspapers, and expert sources. All of them were asked to participate, and those who agreed were interviewed. Like the F.B.I.'s research mentioned above, this is a nonrandom sample. However, like the F.B.I.'s research involv-ing interviews with 29 male serial killers, these seven females come from various geographic areas in the United States, so these offenders illustrate general characteristics of female multiple murderers residing in different correctional facilities around the United States.

### Interview Questions

This study aims to produce information that can help police, re-searchers, parents, and society, by creating profiles of offender types that can assist in identifying active and potential serial offenders, as the F.B.I. research on males has done.

The questionnaire itself was constructed on the basis of prior re-search conducted on male multiple murderers. For instance, *Sexual*

*Homicide: Patterns and Motives* (1988) was examined, a book that discusses the results of the F.B.I.'s research regarding male serial killers. The F.B. I. research has provided significant information about the male multiple murderer's experiences, thoughts, and feelings. Therefore, it is an appropriate source from which to garner questions for this study.

Other researchers have studied the male multiple murderer as well. For example, Ronald Holmes, Ph.D., researched the backgrounds of serial killers and mass murderers, and he is world-renowned in the field of multiple murder. His books were examined to determine what questions would be appropriate for the research. The first source for questions was based upon commonalities found among male offenders in the F.B.I.'s and Dr. Holmes's research.

OUTLINE OF RESEARCH QUESTIONS

**CHILDHOOD**
A. Family
   Socioeconomic status
   Abuse: alcohol, drugs, sexual, emotional
   Play activities
   Religion
B. School
   Grades
   Truancy
   Classroom demeanor
   Friendship
C. Triad of serial murder
   Cruelty to animals
   Fire-setting
   Bedwetting
D. Antisocial behavior
   Fantasy life
   Running away
   Drugs/alcohol
   Sexual activity

E. Physical appearance

**ADOLESCENCE**
A. The aforementioned childhood categories
B. Employment
   Type
   Relationship with boss
   Work habits
C. Pregnancy/Abortion/Miscarriage
D. Birth control
E. Marriage
F. Criminal Activities
   Arrest
   Conviction
G. Children
   How many?
   Custody
   Father
H. Paraphilia
I. Attempted murder
J. Rape
   Offender
   Punishment for offender
   Treatment of victim
K. Car type
L. Fantasy life (as it applies at this age)

**ADULTHOOD**
A. The aforementioned childhood and adolescent categories
B. Fantasy life (as it applies at this age)
C. Murder
   Victim selection
   Relationship with victim
   Motivation
   Method
   Body disposal
   Appearance
   Funeral attendance

**Research Sample**

The research sample involved in this study was comprised of seven Caucasian females. As is consistent with prior studies, many were in care-giving professions which provide access to vulnerable victims. In fact, three of seven were involved in nursing or babysitting while one offender, though not employed as a caregiver, was in charge of her own children when she killed them. Thus, she was acting in a care-giving role at the time of the homicides. The remaining occupations consisted of traditionally feminine jobs: one housewife, one secretary, and two strippers/prostitutes. This coincides with prior research that indicated that female serial killers tend to gravitate toward typically feminine professions (Kirby, 1998).

In addition to the confirmation of occupation, the results affirmed that females tend to be older than males when they commit acts of multiple murder. The average age of the sample was 32.5 at the time of the homicides. This is considerably higher than the average age for male and female homicide offenders in general. It should be noted that the ages of the women varied considerably within the sample. The ages varied from a 17-year-old, to a 58-year-old grandmother. What was remarkable about this research was that the ages were so diverse; it must be emphasized that female multiple murderers can be of any age when

| Table 6-1 displays offender occupation. | | |
|---|---|---|
| **Offender Occupation** | **Number/Total** | **Percent** |
| Babysitter | 2/7 | 28.6 |
| Stripper and Prostitute | 2/7 | 28.6 |
| Nurse | 1/7 | 14.0 |
| Secretary | 1/7 | 14.0 |
| Housewife | 1/7 | 14.0 |

they offend. This is different from males who typically kill within an age range of 25-40 (Cronin, 1996). Thus, the age situation presents a dilemma for law enforcement officials, who cannot limit the pool of suspects based on age and who must override their own beliefs. The female multiple murderer can be very young or very old, and investigation becomes more challenging due to societal expectation (of a certain age range) or lack thereof.

The average number of victims per female was 6, and the total number of known victims was 36. However, during the interviews, one offender admitted to 23 others. It should be noted that at the time of her arrest, this female was 58 years old and was suspected in several other homicides. The average victim age was 48.5, which is older than the average victim-age of male multiple killers; since some women killers choose to commit their acts in nursing homes, this statistic is no surprise. All the victims were Caucasian, and the number of male versus female victims was nearly equal. For the female murderers, there did not appear to be a preference of gender when selecting victims. This is very different from what is known about males.

When examining where and how long female multiple murderers kill, an interesting statistic emerges. The average number of years that the females engaged in murder was 2.14, and consistent with prior re-

| Table 6-2 displays offenders and victims age | | |
|---|---|---|
| Characteristic | Number/Total | Percent |
| Female | 7/7 | 100 |
| White | 7/7 | 100 |
| Caucasian Victims | 36/36 | 100 |
| Male Victims | 20/36 | 56 |
| Female Victims | 16/36 | 44 |
| Average Age | 32.5 | .... |
| Average Number of Victims | 6 | .... |
| Average Victim Age | 48.5 | .... |

search, the women were most commonly found in the southern region of the United States. There is no concrete explanation for why female multiple murderers are more likely to be located in the South, but it is well known that male serial killers are more likely to be located in the Northwest. There has been speculation that old traditions involving poisons have been passed down in the South from generation to generation, and therefore, the traditions may have some connection to why there is an abundance of female multiple murderers in this region (Dr. Gerwe, Personal Communication, 1998).

When examining victim typology, another pattern emerged. Almost all the victims were defenseless in some manner. Either their age prevented the victims from fighting back, or an illness kept the victims immobile. An essentially restrained victim apparently is required for the female multiple murderer to engage in her activities. There was not one instance where a female killed a capable and healthy person. All the victims were powerless, and thus they were unable to harm the females in any attempts at fighting back.

Males select helpless victims as well, but unlike the female offender, the male will often *render* his victim defenseless. This is accomplished through the use of rope, duct tape, or some other type of binding which immobilizes the victim so that the male may inflict whatever injuries he chooses without fight. Thus, the similarity between men and women is limited. Female multiple murderers *select* powerless victims while males *render* their victims helpless. This is a fine distinction but it demonstrates that females actually plan their crimes carefully and seek to minimize their overt involvement in order to protect themselves. It is essential to the female that she be protected and in control of the entire homicidal incident. She does not want to risk being harmed or caught.

**Murder Method**

"Cause of death" is defined as an injury or disease which leads to a physical derangement in the body that brings about a death (DiMaio, 1991). Within this study, two women caused the death of their victims by poisoning, two killed by asphyxiating their victims, two women shot their victims, and one woman stabbed her victims to death. Each woman used only one method for killing her victims and did not attempt any other method.

It is important to note that the female serial killers used less detectable methods (poisons and asphyxia) to kill their victims than the methods used by mass murderers (guns and knives). This is consistent with prior research. In other words, it was difficult for coroners or medical examiners to know the victims were indeed victims of homicide when the killer was a female serial killer. On the other hand, any investigator would recognize the victims of the mass murderer as victims of a homicide. Table 6-3 provides the analysis of murder method.

Overall, the preferred murder method was hands-off, meaning that an instrument was used to kill. This is different from males, who prefer hands-on methods of murder. Male serial killers enjoy touching

| Table 6-3 Murder Method | | |
|---|---|---|
| **Murder Method** | **Number/Total** | **Percent** |
| Asphyxia | | |
|     Strangling | 1/7 | 14.0 |
|     Suffocating | 1/7 | 14.0 |
| Poison | | |
|     At Hospital | 1/7 | 14.0 |
|     In Residence | 1/7 | 14.0 |
| Gunshot | | |
|     Shotgun | 1/7 | 14.0 |
|     .22 Caliber | 1/7 | 14.0 |
| Stabbing | 1/7 | 14.0 |

their victims, and reasons given include terrorizing and degrading the victim (Holmes, 1994). For females, touching their victims is nonessential. The women are more concerned with actually completing the murder act than torturing their victims, and when asked why they chose a hands-off method to kill, the responses were similar. One female mass murderer stated:

> I didn't like getting blood all over everywhere. I mean, I lost it when I shot him (male victim) because he was bleeding on everything. All I wanted to do was wipe it down because I didn't want there to be (evidence) for them (police). I mean, it wasn't like I gave a shit about him (victim). All that mattered to me was keeping my name out of it.

She felt that she could "keep her name out of it" by ensuring that little evidence was left for technicians to collect. This killer was almost hypervigilant regarding hairs, fingerprints, and blood. A female serial killer echoed that sentiment.

> I didn't want to see them (victims) suffer, if that's what you're asking. I'm not that way. I'm the one who took care of my brothers when my father and my mother were either drinking or taking off for, who knows where. I take care of people. That was my job, and that's why I couldn't sit there and watch while they (victims) were suffering. That's when I stepped in and did it, but I didn't want to hurt them.

When asked if she took steps to hide what she was doing, this female replied:

> I'm not stupid, if that's what you're asking. Sure I didn't do it when the other (nurses) were around. It was my private world what I was doing with them. It was like, I could do it,

and nobody else could do it. But no, it wasn't something I went around telling people. I didn't want to be here (prison).

Only one female admitted to having the desire to touch and torture her victims, and she used a knife to kill. She was admittedly a sadist who enjoyed hearing people scream. When she killed one of her female victims, she purposely held the knife over the victim's skin before cutting her in order to see the fear in the victim's eyes. This killer overpowered her victims and rendered them defenseless with stab wounds before selectively cutting them. Like the other females involved in this research, she did select relatively defenseless victims to begin, but she also acted to make them unable to fight back — which parallels male offenders.

Notice the location of the offenders. As previously mentioned, the majority of female serial killers are located in the South. They are diverse in age, and average six victims apiece. When they kill, they choose hands-on methods because, like males, they do enjoy touching their victims. Most often, they are close to those they kill, and in most cases, no one would suspect that they were vicious predators. Unlike males, females prey on men and women equally, taking whoever is most vul-

| Table 6-4 Individual Offender Characteristics | | | | | | | |
|---|---|---|---|---|---|---|---|
| Characteristic | #1 | #2 | #3 | #4 | #5 | #6 | #7 |
| Offender Age | 28 | 17 | 19 | 34 | 35 | 35 | 58 |
| Region of the U.S. | South | South | South | MW | South | MW | West |
| Number of Victims | 5 | 6 | 5 | 2 | 9 | 5 | 11 |
| Murder Method | Stab | Strangle | Shot | Strangle | Poison | Shot | Poison |
| Number of Years Killing | 1 | 2 | 1 | 4 | 1 | 1 | 5 |
| Occupation | SP | CP | PR | Typist | Nurse | HW | CP |

*SP denotes stripper      *PR denotes prostitute
*MW denotes midwest      *HW denotes housewife
* CP denotes care provider

nerable. But like males, they select victims of their own race. Most important was murder method which tended to be covert for the serial killers. By strangling or smothering their victims, they leave little evidence and help ensure that they can continue killing. Mass killers chose weapons of mass destruction, primarily guns. Male mass murderers select guns as well. In this respect, female mass murderers are more similar to male mass killers than female serial killers are to male serial killers.

4

THE PROCESS OF MATURATION

A caterpillar comes forth in the springtime, ready to devour all the green foliage available for consumption before it builds a shelter known as a cocoon. For a specific time period, the caterpillar lives in the cocoon before morphing into winged butterfly. This, for the insect, is a process of maturation, and humans proceed through specific life stages as well. There is a distinct pattern in the childhoods of people who grow up to become mass murderers and serial killers. Unequivocally, certain background factors influence how a multiple murderer is created, and accordingly, how that individual views the world. This process of maturation typically begins at birth and continues until the child reaches adulthood.

Most often, a multiple murderer is situationally vulnerable during childhood, being born into families which are neither loving nor stable; and the lack of family unity creates a sense of disconnect from mainstream society. In this early part of life critical thought and action patterns are established. How does a person view the world? What does a person expect from others? Does the person bond or attach? What is the best way to obtain things? How will the person respond to stress? If a child is not loved and tended, the answers to these questions can be devastating.

Children learn about the world through parental teachings and behavioral examples. Specifically, early experiences shape how an individual views the world and reacts to it under situational stress. As a child grows and develops, the child must attain positive personality traits in order to function well within society when faced with daily stressors such as finances and social relationships (Ressler et al., 1988). The most important of these positive personality traits are autonomy, security, and trust. Research has demonstrated that a child requires consistent and sensitive care giving in order to achieve these meaningful traits (Bowlby, 1944).

The first of these traits, autonomy, is essential in order for a person to function within a societal framework. The autonomous individual is reliable, self-sufficient, and less likely to engage in behaviors that impose upon the rights of others. In order to acquire a sense of autonomy, a child must feel secure. Security is the second positive personality trait. Specifically, a child will only explore and welcome challenges in life when that child feels that a safe environment exists. That way, if problems arise, then the child can return to a safe base when threatened. If a child is not provided with a nurturing environment that makes the child feel safe, then the child will feel uneasy and tentative whenever atypical situations arise. Thus an insecure child will be uncomfortable exploring unknown surroundings and often will act inappropriately when faced with such a position.

But a child needs more than security and autonomy to function. Trust is a trait that is essential for adaptive functioning, and a well-developed sense of security is required in order for a person to trust others. Trust itself grows out of a pattern of consistent caring from a primary caregiver (Bowlby, 1944). That is, a child will learn to expect positive actions from others when he or she has been shown consideration and kindness in early childhood. On the other hand, if a child is not provided with a sense of stability and warmth, that child is unlikely to develop a sense of security and feelings of trust. Without that base from which to build upon, a child cannot grow and function in socially adaptable ways.

There are three primary factors that affect the female multiple murderer's process of maturation. They are:

- Abandonment
- Instability
- Abuse

Each of the aforementioned factors was noted as being highly important and powerful in shaping the female offender. The difference between the offender who survives these three major influences and the person who does not become an offender appears to be the impact or the way that the individual interprets the action. To the killer, the factors become devastating and lifelong scars.

**Abandonment**

As a child, bonding or attaching to a parent is very important since it affects how the child views and interacts with the world in later life. Research has shown that male multiple murderers come from homes where one or both parents abandon the child (Hickey, 1997). Likewise, when the female multiple murderers were asked about positive interactions with family before age five, six were unable to articulate even one positive incident. This is significant, if not unexpected (due to early instability within the family structure).

Early physical abandonment by at least one parent before age 12 was the norm. In fact, two were abandoned by their fathers, two by both parents, and one by her mother, all before they reached age 12. And at least one of their parents deserted the remaining two females once they reached adolescence. The impact was remarkable and had a longitudinal effect. One female serial killer reported her father leaving the family unit when she was 14. She indicated feelings of worthlessness and excessive loneliness because her father was the only person who would talk to her. She had no friends due to her intense level of introversion and obesity, and when her father left, she literally became completely alone.

> Can you think of what it's like to be by yourself every minute? I was, you know, like, uh, this thing that nobody sees. You know what I'm saying? It's like, I want you to understand me. I mean, it's like, as big as I was, it's like I wasn't there. You know? Like, um, like people didn't see me. You know? You remember the old movie the invisible man? It was like he was there, but nobody saw him? It's like, that's me. I'm the invisible girl.

This same female serial killer suffered from obesity and severe acne that contributed to feelings of extreme isolation. So, when she lost her father, she described a feeling of invisibility that in turn evinced high levels of introversion. The abandonment extinguished attachments to others. In other words, when her father left, she could not connect to others. Therefore, she felt completely separated from everyone.

The remaining female mass murderer, though not physically abandoned, was emotionally abandoned. Simply, her abandonment was *de facto* instead of physical. Her father was a drug-using alcoholic who was in a stupor most of his life. When asked how often he was sober and lucid, the subject replied "never." This female reported high stress levels associated with her father's drinking. His role as father was left unfilled, and, having an extremely violent mother, this female was virtually left alone. She, in essence, was abandoned.

The resulting mindset of being left behind traumatizes the female offender to the point that a negative anticipatory effect is created. The young killers learn that when stressful situations arise, there will be no comforting caregiver to respond to the pain (Fonagy et al., 1997). There is no one in the home to give comfort when the usual childhood trials occur. A skinned knee is ignored. A broken heart is left to bleed. Such events cycle repeatedly until the young killers learn to incorporate a preconceived bias of relational hostility and rejection into the personal schema. They come to expect that they will be ignored when injured, so the worldview becomes filled with terror, anger and pain. There is an overriding feeling of social isolation that translates into later social withdrawal and hostility (Meloy, 1988). The entrenched attitude is: I will hurt you before you hurt and/or leave me.

## Siblings

Interestingly, siblings were important. Apparently there is a strong bond with a brother or sister, and even though the women indicated that they felt like outsiders within their families, most stated that they shared a special relationship with a sibling. A sense of protection was accorded either by the sibling or to the sibling meaning that one would stand up for the other. One prime example was noted by a female serial killer who recalled attempting to telephone police when her father was molesting her younger sister. For her behavior, she was choked into unconsciousness with the phone cord. Yet this woman

71

stated that she would do it again because she loved her sister. As the eldest she felt the responsibility to watch over her little sister.

The sibling bond seems to come from the comfort that the brothers and sisters provided to one another during abusive periods. One convicted mass murderer remembered her brother attempting to stand in front of her when her father was beating her. He was knocked unconscious, and the abuse continued. However, this female recalls this memory fondly, and her brother's attempt to protect her meant more to her than whether he succeeded to stop the abuse. To this day, her brother visits her in prison, and she states that they are very close.

There was a contradiction, however, when examining the play activities of these women. Almost all reported acting violently during play activities. This violence was directed at their siblings with whom they felt a special relationship and can only be characterized as extreme and cruel. The brutality consisted of burning either with a cigarette or an appliance, asphyxiating a sibling by pinching the nose and covering the mouth, or wrapping their hands around the sibling's throat. Beating their brothers and sisters was common as well, the instruments being large rocks and sticks. Though each female proclaimed an undying love for their siblings, not one female showed remorse for these violent actions, and they saw no incongruity in their words.

## Instability

The families of female multiple killers never remained in one place for any length of time. This residential instability was cited by all the women as a factor in their failure to form lasting friendships with other children. In fact, one female recalled moving every six months to stay ahead of the law, because her father was a hitman and a member of an outlaw gang. He was known as a "one-percenter." This is a person who is so vicious as to be among the most dangerous of the gang — the top one-percent of the bad. Being a member of this gang kept the family from remaining in one location for any length of time, so uprooting was common.

Being unable to remain in one locale probably contributed to the special kinship felt with the siblings. However, there was a sadness associated with the inability to form friendships with anyone outside the family. When asked if they attempted to make friends, the most common response was: "I knew we *was* moving, so why even try?" Again this demonstrates the preconceived bias and tainted worldview. They expected that they could not form any friendships, so they essentially gave up on attempts to form bonds.

## Abuse

When examining the lives of multiple murderers, there is clearly a pattern of inconsistent and harsh discipline and little if any caring. Therefore, multiple murderers fail to develop positive personality traits because they live with ineffective parents who provide no protection or assistance from trauma. In fact, not only are parents ineffective, but typically, they are brutal abusers who are involved in some type of deviant activity. As a baby, the multiple murderer is subjected to horrific acts of abuse. Instead of warmth and nurturing, the baby is terrorized, resulting in feelings of insecurity and distrust. Abuse whether verbal or physical is the norm (Sears, 1991). To make matters worse, within the multiple killer's environment, the abuse and inconsistent discipline have been found to result in violent behavior in later life (Wilson & Herrnstein, 1985).

Furthermore, in these homes, there is a marked amount of neglect that fosters a deep-seated distrust within the child. Distrust results

from inadequate and often cruel parenting techniques that include torturing and beating the child (Egger, 1997). As the child grows, this distrust spills over into resentment and intense levels of anger. It becomes
difficult for the young killer to relate to the world because the individual has undergone a unique transformation. Since the individual did not
receive love or caring while growing up, he or she begins to devalue the
concept of attaching or bonding with others (Bowlby, 1979). In other
words, the young killer views love and caring as unimportant because
he or she never received affection. In the killers' minds, warmth and
attachment are devalued to the point of oblivion (Geberth, 1997).

The killer's life becomes devoid of social attachment due to self-
imposed isolation. Researchers have found that even when the young
killer wanted to make connections with other people, the offender
would be lost as to how one forms relationships with another person
(Sears, 1991). The offender is not able to sustain any type of relationship
for any length of time due to overwhelming feelings of anger, loneliness,
and stimulation-seeking (Geberth, 1997). Multiple murderers, literally,
are emotional wrecks who cannot fit into a social network. To compli-
cate the situation, the killers observe others who have had nurturing
families where affectional bonding took place, and it becomes difficult
to watch others have what was never available to him or her (Norris,
1988).

### Anger Builds and Builds

The hatred for others and the violence that has been assimilated
as normal begins to dominate this persona. The world is seen as a place
filled with people who are devalued (Geberth, 1997). The multiple murderers fail to bond with family or make attachments to society, so there
is no parameter of empathy to constrain the individual from commit-

ting atrocious acts. Those outside of the killer's family have no impact on the offender because the offender refuses to get emotionally bonded with anyone. Thus a sense of right and wrong (morality) is not programmed into these individuals.

When looking at females, the resemblance to the patterns in the lives of male offenders was incredible. All the women involved in this research reported growing up in violent households, experiencing some form of physical, sexual, or emotional indignity. Abuse was pronounced and prolonged, meaning that the acts were extreme and occurred over long periods of time. Even though the physical and sexual abuse was pronounced, all seven women cited *emotional* abuse as their worst experience while growing up. The emotional component took the form of making the child feel unwanted and unloved, and one female suggested that it was so severe as to make her insane. Because of the terrible emotional torture, the women were made to feel like the black sheep of the families. They were outsiders within their own groups, and such devastating feelings led to high levels of introversion.

It was not uncommon for females who grow up to become multiple murderers to live with people who were verbally abusive. Like the physical and sexual abuse, verbal assaults were inconsistent but severe. Typical waves of verbal attacks included such statements as:

— There is no such thing as love, and even if there was, nobody would love *you*.
— If you had a brain, you'd find a way to ruin it.
— I hate you.
— I'm going to kill you.
— You're a worthless fat piece of shit.
— Don't open your mouth. You'd only say something stupid.
— Why can't you go somewhere and die?
— Nobody likes you.
— You should kill yourself.

These are the words that created feelings of devastation within the young female multiple murderers, and it must be noted that the statements were repetitive and continued throughout childhood and adolescence. These were not one-time occurrences. When asked why the words were so prominent in their memories, the women indicated that scars from physical abuse heal, but the emotional scars remain. As one female serial killer stated "the emotional shit drives you crazy. I mean, who the hell is going to believe you?"

But beyond the verbal threats, almost all of the women reported sexual abuse beginning before age five. The abuse consisted of vaginal rape, anal assault, oral sex , and penetration with objects such as pipes and sticks. The assaults were brutal, often leading to vaginal or anal bleeding on at least one occasion. Males in the households were most often the perpetrators of the sexual abuse while male relatives were closely linked with rape as well. The sexual attacks continued for at least one year, but most of the women reported the length of time being three to four years.

Add physical abuse to this mix, and one can begin to see a deadly soup of bottled emotions. Physical abuse was as prevalent as sexual attacks, but in most instances, the abuse was delivered by a female in authority. Strangely, this coincides with what is known about the male multiple killer who typically grows up in household run by a domineering female (Ressler et al., 1988). The physical abuse consisted of beatings, cutting, burning, and biting.

The violence can only be characterized as sadistic. The randomness of the attacks created constant levels of fear. Because the acts were seemingly without provocation, the women were in a virtual state of hyper-vigilance. All seven women reported being continually watchful due to the feeling that some type of assault could occur at any time because they never knew when a parent might strike them. It is well documented that male multiple murderers come from homes where discipline is inconsistent (Holmes & Holmes, 1998), and apparently, females suffer from a similar environment. There was no rhyme or reason to being tortured, and the women never knew when pain was coming. A parent's good mood could turn bad in a flash, so there was always a fear that beatings could come at any moment. As one female mass murderer stated:

> My dad would pick me up and carry me to the furnace, and I knew what was coming. He'd take my socks off and put my feet on the side (of the furnace). I'd be kicking and screaming, but it never stopped him. I remember hearing the sizzle of my feet burning.

Another female mass murderer convicted of killing five people recalled how her mother would torture her. There was nothing in particular that provoked the abuse, but the ritual was always the same:

> She'd get that knife and chase me, uh, you know? I tried to run, but . . . She'd slash at my calves like this (female made a slicing motion in the air) when I fell. It got so bad I wore pants so, uh, it was like no one could see them (the scars).

This same female reported experiencing hyper-vigilance since the attacks were unprovoked and occurred at random. Again, the inconsistency of abuse created high levels of stress that created greater self-reliance and introversion. The stories were similar for each research subject. One female serial killer recounted one of the worst beatings she ever received from her stepmother. This event was documented through hospital records and involved a two-by-four board.

I came home from school, and she was in *that* mood. If I'd have known that, I never would have said nothing to her. Because when she was like that, you didn't say nothing to her, you know? She'd tear at us kids, mainly me, because she didn't want me. They [the stepmother and father] wanted my little sister, and the only way they could get her was to take me in. It was like, hey, I was the black sheep, and she [stepmother] never let me forget it. She'd beat me up and lock me in the closet. And it was dark, and I couldn't see anything. I don't know how long she'd leave me in there, but I'd make up this other life where I was different. I wanted to kill them, you know? That day I came home from school, I must've said something wrong because she hauled off and hit me in the back of the head with a board. All I remember was seeing her with the two by four, and the next thing I knew, it went dark after that. You know she never came to see me at the hospital? I could've died for all she cared. How's that for love?

| Table 6-6 Family Background Characteristics | | |
|---|---|---|
| **Characteristic** | **Number/Total** | **Percent** |
| Family Problems | | |
|     Drug/Alcohol Abuse | 5/7 | 71.0 |
|     Psychiatric History | 1/7 | 14.0 |
|     Criminal History | 1/7 | 14.0 |
| Abuse/Neglect | | |
|     Physical Abuse | 7/7 | 100 |
|     Physical Abuse > 1 Year | 7/7 | 100 |
|     Psychological Abuse | 7/7 | 100 |
|     Sexual Abuse | | |
|       During Childhood | 7/7 | 100 |
|       During Adolescence | 5/7 | 71.0 |
|     Sexual Abusers | | |
|       Non-Relatives | 4/7 | 57.0 |
|       Relatives | 2/7 | 29.0 |
| Hyper-vigilance | 7/7 | 100 |
| Inconsistent Discipline | 6/7 | 87.0 |

So, from infancy, the female multiple murderer learns that pain is expected, and there is no protection. One female convicted of 9 murders stated:

> I remember because they (natural parents) wouldn't let me forget. My father liked (little) girls, and every night he'd come into my room with his pants undone, and I knew what that meant. There wasn't no one to stop it. My mother was a drunk who'd pass out by seven (o'clock). There wasn't anything to do but do it."

This convicted killer was repeatedly raped, vaginally, orally, and anally from age two. She said that it was from this early experience that she learned not to trust anybody. Furthermore, she was adamant that being raped made her feel miserable and helpless, and she vowed as she got older never to feel that way again, "no matter what it took."

So, consistent patterns of abandonment and horrific abuse characterize the backgrounds of females who grow up to become multiple murderers. In the process of maturation the sexual, physical, and emotional components are powerful influences. Horrific acts of abuse, on an inconsistent basis, lead to high levels of introversion and hypervigilance. In other words, the young females learn to trust no one and to always be vigilant for violence. Thus, they become highly accustomed to feeling uneasy. These feelings become an integral part of their later lives. As they mature, they become ever-more isolated partially in response to their weight issues. They cannot make friends because they feel like outsiders, and all recall terrible teasing because of their weight. Being afraid and feeling like they do not fit in adds to increased feelings of distrust toward others. This leads to an inability to form bonds. Additionally, the young female killers change residences frequently because of parental instability. This minimizes the child's ability to attach or form lasting friendships. Thus bonding is almost nonexistent.

**Physicality: Appearance and Multiple Murder**

It was interesting to note that physically, while growing up, female multiple murderers resembled one another in more than one way. In other words, they had similar appearances. Of the seven women interviewed for this research, all seven acknowledged suffering from obesity as young children and during adolescence. Each woman recalled being the largest in her school class in grade school, and the weight problem continued through early adolescence. At the same time, the young females were not tall. In fact, all seven females involved in this study stand no taller than 5'5, and this height was reached during adolescence. Height, therefore, did not correlate with excess weight. This data differs from what is known about male multiple murderers, for males typically do not have a history of obesity in their backgrounds. The women stated that weight had been an issue for them all of their lives, and they struggle with eating problems on a daily basis.

It is not surprising to hear that female multiple murderers did not exercise and play with other children. Instead of engaging in outdoor games involving running and jumping, the young female multiple murderers remained indoors, in their rooms, where they enjoyed solitary play activities. The most common reason given was that they felt that they did not fit in with other children, so they avoided contact with kids whenever possible. This coincides with research on male multiple murderers who also enjoyed solitary play activities as well (Ressler et al., 1988). The weight issue was far-reaching and created feelings of low self-worth and animosity toward those outside the home. For their obesity, the young women suffered taunting and teasing which was persistent and cruel. Again, this reinforced the preferred desire to spend time alone.

In addition to having weight problems, most females suffered from severe acne in late childhood/early adolescence. The acne was severe enough to leave physical scars on the faces of the adult women, who to this day feel self-conscious about it. When asked how long they had suffered from acne, the women acknowledged that it persisted through their teen-aged years. Because they were obese and had acne-covered faces, they were constantly teased and harassed by both family and school children.

This led to further feelings of isolation that forced the females to retreat into a fantasy life. In the beginning, the mental cognitions were mere escapes from outside pain, and in those fantasies, happiness was the key. Initial fantasies involved playing, growing up, and marrying into a perfect life. Because the fantasies were pleasant, they were preferred to reality. Spending time away from other people turned into a pattern that, once established, would not be broken.

Physical appearance had a significant impact on the females. Because they were heavy and acne-prone, they were outcasts who had little choice but to isolate in order to protect themselves. It should be noted that six women had average or better intelligence as determined

| Table 6-5 Childhood Attributes | | |
|---|---|---|
| **Childhood Attributes** | **Number/Total** | **Percent** |
| Obesity | 7/7 | 100 |
| Both Parents Present Upon Birth | 7/7 | 100 |
| Good Verbal Skills as Evidenced During Interview | 6/7 | 86 |
| Stable Family Income — At least One Parent Working | 4/7 | 57 |
| Teen-Aged Acne | 3/7 | 43 |

by personal interviews and existing data. This was an important factor in the backgrounds of the women involved in the research. They were intelligent enough to realize that they were different from other children, and this led to further feelings of separation.

## Family Functioning

From outward appearances, female multiple murderers initially come from stable homes. That is, both parents were present during the first six months of the child's life, and most women came from families where at least one parent had a steady job and income. However, upon examining court records and conducting the interviews, it was determined that both parents were present for only a brief period in the child's life, and when one parent abandoned the child, the steady income disappeared as well.

Furthermore, family interaction and attachment was described by the women as either dysfunctional or nonexistent. There was no consistent pattern as to birth order, but in most instances, the female was an unplanned pregnancy. Though there was no one dominant religion in the backgrounds of these females, the women stressed the importance placed on going to church each Sunday. Apparently the family unit, though low on attachment, placed a premium on church attendance. For those women who attended church regularly, all stated that it was mandatory that they do so. If they objected, they were beaten.

In all cases, at least one parent experienced problems and stresses that inhibited the ability to parent a child effectively. These problems exhibited themselves within the family unit. Almost all of the women reported alcohol/drug abuse by at least one parent on multiple occasions. The abuse was so severe that five women stated that they could not recall a time when at least one parent was not under the influence of drugs or alcohol. Furthermore, parental impairment did not stop with controlled substances. For example, one female grew up in a home where a parent suffered from a psychiatric disorder, and one female had a father who was a criminal. The remaining parents had no significant criminal histories.

The components of abuse, abandonment, appearance, and inadequate family functioning interrupt and permanently mar the process of maturation so that the females who emerge from these homes are ill equipped to function in society. They are distrustful introverts who prefer spending time alone. They are not able to get past these childhood indignities.

These concrete background factors should be noted when a female is suspected in acts of multiple murder. Though they are not in and of themselves predictors of violence, they can act as building blocks to multiple homicide. A thorough examination of a suspect's background can aid detectives in building a court case. Further study should concentrate on these characteristics and their relationship to future violence.

## 5

FROM FANTASY TO REALITY

### Living in Daydreams

Daydreaming is an escape into a mental realm where reality has little meaning. It is a journey of cognition and desire, a desperate attempt to claim what does not exist in the functioning world. Everyone daydreams. Children retreat into their play worlds while sitting in a classroom and the adult worker may pretend to listen when instead the attention is diverted into a more pleasurable realm. The significance of daydreaming in homicide, specifically multiple homicide, is devastatingly important.

It is well known that male multiple murderers fantasize about killing. From a young age, males conjure images of brutality and violence that they repeat in their minds whenever they are stressed. It was the hypothesis of this author that females would have similar mental functioning, and during the course of the interviews, a fascinating theme emerged. Not only do females enjoy violent fantasies, but they begin having them at a very young age. All seven of the women interviewed admitted to a high level of introversion that led to an intrusive and reiterative thought pattern (violent fantasies). These violent fantasies typically began in early adolescence, though one female acknowledged images of murder at age seven.

From an early age, the female engages in escapist thoughts. As one considers the abusive turmoil that the young girls endure, there is a specific reason for the mental retreat. In the beginning, the thoughts tend to be harmless, centering more on a perfect life than anything vicious. In the dreams there is a husband who is loving, children, and a wonderful home. Life is incredible, and in that world, no can hurt her.

However, eventually the female must return to reality, and the abuse and abandonment hit a nerve. So her daydreams change. They become more elaborate and centered on violence. In the fantasy, the female harms someone, and at first, this is pleasing and produces a calming effect. However, hiding in one's mind is only a temporary fix, and when reality strikes again, the pain and feelings of helplessness that drove her to the fantasy return. The elaborate cognitions (intense fantasies) serve as a displacement for feelings of pent up rage and frustration. Being small and unable to defend against rape and brutality, the women feel they have no choice but to run into their thoughts. They use the daydreams as a conduit to tranquility. Simply, these women use violent daydreams to relieve stress.

Somewhere along the line, the fantasies become worse.

As the young future killer becomes more isolated, from family as well as schoolmates, fantasy becomes more important, even more important than human interaction (Ressler et al., 1988). After awhile, the individual comes to prefer autoerotic (self-arousal) activities, and as such, feels profoundly different from other people. Because the killer grows up in situations where he or she spends unusual amounts of time alone, this throws the killer into further isolation where a fantasy takes over. Instead of dreaming of how life will improve as the aging process occurs, the young killer takes out frustrations inside his or her thoughts by making the self all-powerful in dreams.

Concentrating on these fantasies becomes easy because of general isolation. All seven women reported being isolated from others. This isolation was physical as well as emotional. In fact, spending excessive time alone was a primary behavioral indicator for female multiple murderers involved in this research. All stated that an inordinate amount of their time was spent alone while in childhood, adolescence, and adulthood. This time was filled with violent daydreams.

These fantasies became all consuming to the female offender who reacted to the grotesque cognitions by erecting barriers to the outside world. As she became more entrenched into a rich and violent fantasy life, the female multiple murderer reported increased stress levels brought about by her realization that her thought patterns were divergent from mainstream thought. In response, the female multiple killer became ever more isolated. The female multiple murderer fantasized about killing, and when she had contact with others, she realized that her thought pattern was unique. So, in order to avoid the feelings of dissonance created by human interaction, she isolated herself and began retreating further into her own mind.

As the female multiple murderer became more secluded, an interesting change took place. At first, her violent fantasies simply involved the act of murder. That is, of those who admitted to violent fantasies, all stated that those fantasies simply started with the murder of another human being. There were no specific plans or elaborate body disposal methods. These fantasies did include a murder weapon. One woman reported fantasies involving killing with a gun, while five others stated that their fantasies entailed some form of asphyxia (suffocation or strangulation). Lastly, one woman refused to answer this fantasy question.

Furthermore, the initial fantasy lives of the female murderers were not directed at specific individuals. Six subjects stated that, initially, their mental violence was directed at nameless bodies. Any person would be acceptable in the role of murder victim. Thus, the initial fantasies were directed at the elderly, men, women, and children. It was only after a period of several months that these women reported fixating their violent cognitions on a specific individual, usually someone they knew.

All but one of the subjects noted increasing violence within their fantasies.

Remarkably, the women were able to recall their fantasies in vivid detail. The women were able to recite violent mental images that corresponded with how they eventually killed. Once they chose a specific method of murder in their fantasies, that method ended up being the method used to eventually kill.

As they got closer to committing homicide, the women experienced more intense and specific fantasies involving pre-crime, crime, and post-crime behaviors. Immediately prior to committing murder, the female multiple murderer experienced elaborate and obsessively detailed thoughts that invaded every facet of her life. There were very detailed fantasies of how to make a victim vulnerable as well as how to make the homicide look like a natural death. These thoughts were all consuming. Every detail (how to avoid being apprehended) was thought out and incorporated into her fantasy. When the completed fantasies were repeated several times, the females took steps to commit the homicide. In other words, once the cognitions became rote, the female multiple murderer began to prepare for murder.

They read. And they read a lot. Just what they read makes their crimes more heinous. Female multiple killers read materials to educate themselves about murder and forensic pathology. They visit their local libraries and check out books about poisons, autopsy procedures and police procedures. The admitted purpose was to learn how to kill without being detected. After reading, they then introduce their knowledge into their fantasies. They actually incorporate forensic knowledge into their fantasy lives. For instance, one serial killer who strangled one victim admitted to changing her murder method to suffocation upon learning that strangling leaves marks on the neck.

It is after the female multiple murderer begins educating herself that her repeated acts of homicide begin. She is confident in her new-found expertise. Since she had rehearsed this thought-pattern repeatedly and educated herself, she feels self-assured about her ability to carry out the violent acts that consume her mind. For the first time, she believes that she can do something that very few people can, and she believes that she will be successful in eluding detection. Once she attains this confidence, she chooses a victim who is close and defenseless, and she acts out her fantasy in precise detail.

Of the seven women involved in this research, two killed by using poison, two killed by asphyxiating their victims, one shot her victims, while the seventh stabbed her victims. All used the murder method about which they had fantasized. For instance, the female mass murderer who enjoyed sadistic sex involving knives used a knife to stab her victims to death. Similarly, the female serial killer who fantasized about asphyxiating her victims actually smothered and strangled her six victims.

For a brief time following the homicides, there is a feeling of elation.

For once in their lives, they have succeeded, and they are the predators. They felt successful at making their dreams into reality, and all-powerful while committing the murders. However, this euphoria quickly dissipates leaving the female to feel lonely and isolated once more. Then the violent fantasies continue and become ever more incessant. The female is faced with the prospect of getting caught for her action, yet she feels no remorse. She just doesn't want to go to prison.

This is the mindset of the multiple murderer. After delving into this world, one may ask what kind of person thinks these thoughts? Just what are these female killers?

## Evil Minds

What is evil? Can it possibly exist? There are many people who would argue that anyone who commits serial or mass murder must be depraved and vile, components that comprise the notion of evil itself. The idea indicates that a normal person could not ever act out in such a vicious way, so those who do commit horrible acts of violence must certainly be different from the rest of society. They must be evil. But is it enough to simply regard acts that are heinous as crimes of inhuman monsters? Certainly there are those who prefer the dark side in life. Likewise, multiple murderers seek to obliterate their victims, and in many cases, they do so because they enjoy killing. Clearly this suggests a penchant for being bad or even evil. However, there are no tests as the notion of evil is intangible and cannot be studied. Thus, scholars can banter back and forth and never come to an exact conclusion as to whether evil does exist. So, it was put to the offenders themselves, serial killers and mass murderers to answer that question. Would the killers themselves be able to articulate the notion of evil, or better yet, would they acknowledge the existence of evil?

When asked these questions, there were very interesting answers that help create a picture into the mind of a multiple murderer. A female who was convicted of five murders (but admitted to attempting many more) spoke freely about the concept of evil. In fact, she was the one who brought up the subject. She said:

> Being human means we are both good and evil, and in order
> to be balanced and healthy human beings, we must become
> aware of our own needs, desires, competencies, and limita-
> tions. Without such knowledge, we feel what? Uncertainty,
> inadequate, meaningless, frustrated, desperate, alienated,
> and all of those other ills that live in Pandora's Box. What
> happens when we get caught up in our own confusion? I
> never understood my capacity for compassion until I started
> killing. Hate, rage, and anger are better places to be than the
> defeat we feel underneath the hate.

This offender was asked if she believed in evil, and her response
was "of course." She felt that in order to be complete, a person has to
recognize both sides of the personality. In other words, a person must
understand that he or she can be dark as well as light, that we as human beings have free will and can make choices. Some of these choices
are bad while others are beneficial, yet there is a possibility for either
even within the most chaste human. But notice that this female makes
no attempt within her words to fight off the dark side. She embraces it
openly and has a twisted belief that she was only able to be compas-
sionate after she killed. Simply, after killing, she could understand another person's pain, or so she would like people to believe. In investigating her background, it was discovered that this woman had attempted to kill over nine other men through stabbing and shooting. It
was only through pure luck that her victims managed to survive. In
fact, she stabbed her male victims close to the heart, and certainly, she
intended to kill them. She freely admitted that.

The other women were quick to point out that darkness did exist
in the world, but they did not feel that they were evil. Other than the
one offender who acknowledged her part in evil, the remaining women

stated that it was other people who were evil. They were victims of cir-cumstances, not cold-hearted monsters who killed for enjoyment.

It was interesting that they did, however, admit to being "mean." All of the women realized that they were mean children who grew up into mean adults. They appeared to be more comfortable with this term than the notion of evil. When asked how mean was different from evil, one female serial killer simply said "evil is damnation. It's like you're finished. But mean is something else. Like its not so bad."

It is here that the pervasive theme in all of the interviews emerged. There was a terrifying lack of sympathy for those who were killed and those left behind. The dead were mere objects to be relegated to a posi-tion of nothingness, and nothing was what the victims became. There was absolutely *no* sympathy expressed for the victims or their families. Period. This reinforced the idea that victims to such killers are noth-ings. Even the victims' names are long forgotten, as they become num-bers in society, a statistic of the damned. If you think about it, you are sure to be able to name five serial killers, but can you name the victims of those killers?

So does evil exist?

No one can quantify it exactly. There are vague notions. Acts that are too horrid to speak. But does that qualify as evil? Perhaps the an-swer lies in the thoughts of these killers. For a person to repeatedly concentrate on various ways to make a human suffer and die must mean there is something different, something horribly wrong. To know this is to know that we must take steps to prevent the *thoughts* before we can stop the killing. That brings us back to an early preventive in-tervention, which is a must if we are to conquer multicide.

Killing multiple victims is inexcusable, but in some ways it is un-derstandable, when glancing at the histories of these offenders. This is only to say that there are reasons why multiple murder occurs. In order to stop the crime, one must understand the reasons. To put it simply, children who are unloved, abused, and abandoned will not be stellar citizens. When one loads garbage into a box, one cannot expect to open it up and find a rose.

# 6

## THE SADISTIC FEMALE MULTIPLE MURDERER

## Pain and Fury

It was warm that spring, unseasonably warm for the heart of the new season. It was hot, and the misty sun bore through that late Saturday afternoon as if it were a June day in the depths of the Florida Everglades. Maddie* had a gun. Lisa* had a sharpened knife. And they were both women with a taste for terror. The irony escaped them — how spring evinces thoughts of life and rebirth after months of a dark and depressing winter. In fact, Maddie and Lisa never even noticed the bright-green baby buds clinging to the branches of the reborn tree limbs. Forsythia had bloomed weeks before, and the scent of juvenile flowers spread through the air.

Drugs would play a part as they so often do, but it wasn't drugs that stoked the flames of murder that Saturday night. Hatred was there. And more importantly, a sadistic fantasy life had run amok. Maddie and Lisa had hate in their hearts, and their destinies would quickly unfold like a used towel tossed to the floor.

Serial killers and mass murderers have been known to work in pairs throughout the country, just like Lisa and Maddie. And when two diabolical minds come together, it is as if the devil was dancing in their eyes. One of the most heinous cases was that of Charles Ng and his partner Leonard Lake who in the state of Washington reportedly killed thirteen people with gunshot wounds to the head (Holmes & Holmes, 1994). These two men killed whomever struck their fancy, and their likes encompassed both males and females. Together, they would stalk people through trading post ads in local newspapers. The hunt was simple. They would scour the classified ad section of the local newspaper and call to select a victim. Selling items in the newspaper wouldn't seem dangerous, but if Leonard Lake and Charles Ng came calling, all sales would be final.

Predators are everywhere, and in the case of Charles Ng and Lake, if a seller was alone, the sale became a death sentence. At one time, they captured a husband, a wife, and their baby. Lake and Ng had a house in a remote area. No neighbors for miles. No person for miles. No way out. In the wilderness, the husband was quickly shot in the head, and upon his death, the two killers asked the wife if she would prefer to die or become their sex slave. To 'sweeten' the pot, so she would agree to degrading sexual acts, the killers held her baby hostage. "I don't want to die," she replied. And the two men took that as a yes to their horrid question. She was tortured, broken, then finally killed. They videotaped her torment for their own amusement, and her suffering is forever captured on a thin piece of film. Of course the baby never even had a chance (Geberth, 1998).

*Femmes fatales* are no different from their twisted male counterparts, and as one returns to that Saturday night when Lisa and Maddie ran amok in the beautiful springtime air, an eerie fear starts to grip the mind. Lisa was a 27-year-old stripper who had no documented history of violence, but proof is an elusive commodity. She was known to use and buy drugs, and most of the time after using up her money, she'd sell her body for some quick cash. She revealed a past filled with sadomasochism and grotesque violence. "I like to hurt people," she said with a smile and a twinkle in her eye. She liked sex where she could beat and whip her partners to the point of making her partner bleed. "I like to draw blood to get excited."

And this desire to hurt must have been the motivation for the murders of five people.

Maddie was another story. She was 22 and ready to kill anything that made her the slightest bit angry. She'd been in and out of police stations most of her life, a life filled with terror and torture. She was raised amongst an outlaw motorcycle gang who made mainstream depictions of biker-life seem tame. Her mother was a non-person who acted as if the young girl were nonexistent. And her father was even worse. When he was around, he'd pass her around to other members of the gang to use her as an experimental sex toy. This was where her state of rage and helplessness began. From the rapes forward, Maddie formed a hatred of human beings.

While she was growing up, Maddie had not only killed animals, but she had tried to kill people as well. Being a part of an outlaw motorcycle gang, she was taught how to kill using a knife at the age of seven. And she had a history of knifing and shooting people. During our interview, she said that every time she stabbed or shot someone "I aimed for the heart to kill them." She had no qualms about killing. She simply felt that it was her right because she had been so wronged.

Given their backgrounds, it wasn't too surprising that these women were on a course of destruction. Together they were lesbian lovers, drawn to each other in a twisted 'love' game involving sadistic sex and painful domination. Lisa was the sadist who took delight in "bringing blood to a person." Maddie, who describes herself as more feminine than butch, had taken on the role of being Lisa's keeper. She called Lisa a 'gutter slut,' a term used to describe a hooker who does anyone, anytime, and anywhere. In other words, a whore who is not choosy about a who a client may be.

"That was Lisa," Maddie said in our interview. "I felt that she was beneath me. She was a street whore. You know, she stood on the corners and sold her ass. And I felt that's not the way you do things. I was real protective of her. So I developed this love/hate relationship with her."

Maddie was known to have a horrible temper and she'd use it as a tactic to bully Lisa and everyone around her. She was a fighter, having been taught to knife and hit others during her days with her father's gang. So, Lisa relied on her for protection, even though sometimes Maddie turned violent on her as well. As an example of how they lived, Maddie described an incident that occurred at a biker convention. Essentially, this story sums up her relationship with Lisa.

There was a biker convention, you know, where they all get together and party and set up booths. They'd sell things; you know, just bullshit like that. There'd be tit flashing. You know you'd get up on the stand and show your titties and jam. I went to the rally with an Armed Warrior. He was a member of the Armed Warriors, a motorcycle gang. And I had two cousins who were in the Peacemakers, another gang. These were two different 'clubs'. All right, I walked by the campfire, going to get some beer. And Lisa's sister called me a bitch, so I sucker punched her. She fell in the fire, and these bikers started toward us. You know when women fight at a place like this, they get pushed to the road like pit bulls. Other members make them fight. They bet on them and everything. Well, Lisa was there, and there was another girl with me and this Armed Warrior. You know, it was a three-way sex thing. We'd do this guy together, you know. And anyway, when we're walking away toward this road, Lisa comes up behind me and went for my legs. So I hit her a couple of times, like a reflex, and she was knocked out. And I kicked her as she was going down. She had to have five stitches in her head and five stitches in her chin.

Their violent lifestyles made that spring Saturday almost inevitable. On the fateful day, Lisa and Maddie were ready to explode. They had been up for a three days shooting drugs at Maddie's drug gallery. In fact, Maddie was known throughout the area to use and sell drugs, and she had a house, otherwise known as her gallery, where junkies would come to get a hit of whatever made them fly. Cocaine. Heroine. You name it; she had it.

And after using drugs for three days, their inner hatred for the world began to turn into violent fantasy and eventually reality. They were both feeling helpless because of family and money troubles, so in a drug stupor, they made their way to an apartment complex for the city's poor where they had sold themselves to men willing to pay for sex. The residents were typically alcoholics or drug users who squandered any money they would get on a quick high. The men would slip money to Maddie and Lisa in exchange for various sexual fantasies, and a 73-year-old named Jake was known for his taste in young women. It was a sexual turn-on for the old man, and Maddie confided that he had asked to watch her and Lisa have oral sex when his wife Carrie was away.

On that spring Saturday, Jake had been drinking, and when Lisa and Maddie asked him for money, he refused them. The drugged-up women weren't accustomed to rejection, especially not from an old man, and their anger had forced them into a readiness to act out. Lisa and Maddie, worn from the drugs, violently screamed at Jake.

"We're not leaving without the money," said Lisa.

Jake's wife Carrie called the police around 4 p.m., and police arrived to find the intoxicated group arguing. It was a domestic-type dispute, but the police officers dutifully escorted Lisa and Maddie from the building.

"They told us to stay away, you know, not to go back," said Maddie during our interview. "They told us to stay away, but we were gonna get that money. I mean we knew they didn't have any money. Shit none of us had money, but it was like, we were gonna get it from them." Maddie paused and shrugged. " I guess we should've stayed away."

Lisa parroted Maddie's words.

"We wanted money," said Lisa in an interview. "They didn't have it, but it was like we wanted it."

So, as soon as the police left, the two made their way back to Jake's apartment. And Jake let them in. What they didn't know was that Jake had also been drinking, and he was feeling angry too. As they yelled and screamed at him in an attempt to obtain his money, he pulled out his gun and pointed it directly at Maddie's head. Lisa pulled out her knife and slipped it underneath his chin in order to protect Maddie.

"Give her the gun," said Lisa.

So Jake handed Maddie his weapon, but he did not anticipate what would occur next.

Pettiness is said to drive the most inhumane acts, and what these two killers proceeded to do was both cruel and completely heartless. Jake's suffering would destroy even the toughest spirit, for the pain that was about to take place would be legendary, even to those who handle these crimes on a daily basis.

There are those who would say that emotional torture is far worse than any physical harm that can be inflicted on a victim, for cuts and bruises on the body eventually heal. But the mind has a way of remembering. The *exact* feelings come back whenever a person recalls a painful memory. This is why mental torture is so cruel, because it stays with us, and this is how Lisa and Maddie decided to torture their victims.

As the killers recall, they ordered Jake and Carrie out to the next-door neighbor's apartment. Maddie said "We left their (Jake and Carrie) place, you know, so we leave well enough alone. And we go next door where some friends are working on their car. So we started drinking with them, and she (Lisa) got the knife out again, playing with it. I don't know what her obsession was with it." At this point Jake and Carrie were joined by Marie, Phil, and Andy. All three were nearly fifty years old, and, like Jake and Carrie, they were frightened of the two knife-wielding women. Maddie and Lisa ordered all five people to get into the back seat of Jake's car. Each of the five victims had reached a point where they doubted their physical abilities, and they didn't think that they could get away.

The story changes in the minds of the killers at this point, each one providing a different view of how those five people got into the back seat of the car. Lisa said that they were just going for a joy ride while Maddie places blame on her accomplice for forcing the five victims into the back of the car. Their stories may differ, yet one fact is undeniable. Five human beings got into the back seat of the car, and not one of them came out alive.

As the killers recounted it, they took the middle aged and elderly victims to a dirt covered field and ordered them out of the car. They were told to lay face down on the field. Then one by one, Maddie shot at them. Almost at the same time, Lisa stabbed them where they lay in the dirt.

"She only nicked them," said Lisa. "They weren't hurt much."

Along the same thought pattern, her partner with the gun stated that her accomplice had cut the victims as they lay in the field. Remarkably, despite the chilling injuries sustained by the victims, the two killers were far from finished. It was as if the five human beings had become like the toy mouse that the cat bats back and forth with its paws. None of the injuries had been fatal, but they were all bleeding from their wounds. Maddie and Lisa ordered the victims to get up and get back into the car that had brought them there.

Maddie relayed the events of her life and described the murders to this author:

> She (Lisa) had told Phil to take his shirt off, and she was wiping blood off Marie. Marie's throat had been cut a little bit. She was bleeding, so I got mad then. This part is difficult for me to talk about because I haven't worked through this all yet. I remember running around the side of the car, and I remember shooting her. And I guess after that, two or three were shot there, but they didn't die. I remember leaving the field, and I was alternating between reality and fantasy.

Lisa confirmed this part of the night to this author during an interview. As the victims leaned backwards into the seat, their blood covered the interior of the car. Lisa said that she grew angry when this happened. "I had Phil take his shirt off to keep him from getting blood all over the car. The blood excited me. I didn't want him getting blood all over the car."

Lisa and Maddie sat quietly for a few moment as their victims bled quietly in the back seat. They hadn't decided what they were going to do next, but life had no meaning to the two women, and so, neither did the lives of those five victims.

"I was alternating between reality and fantasy," said Maddie. "Even though it happened over a period of hours, it seemed to go by fast. It was like a dream."

To the victims, it was more like a nightmare gone very, very wrong. But there wasn't one thing that the aged victims could or would do. The pair admitted that as they looked at each other, they knew they were going to kill them.

"We did Marie first," said Maddie. "We told her to get out of the car, and that's where I shot her in the back of the head. And Lisa stabbed her."

Lisa recalls not just stabbing Marie, but slicing her neck as well. "I stabbed her, I don't know how many times. It was several times, and I cut her throat from behind."

Neither woman knows how it happened, but after they had shot and stabbed Marie, they returned to the car and drove off dragging Marie on the car's tailpipe for several blocks while she was still alive. They didn't take the time to stop the car and remove her.

Such atrocious acts are not unheard of in the world of multiple murder. Dragging Marie behind the car is similar to a brutal murder committed by two male serial killers who captured, tortured and killed teen-aged females in their specially equipped van. Their goal was to kill a female teenager for every teenage year. That is, kill a girl of nineteen, eighteen, and so forth. The crimes of Lawrence Bittaker and Roy Norris are among the most gruesome and horrific of all serial murder cases.

The lures were simple: drugs or a ride to a specified location. In the early 1980's, it was still commonplace for young women to hitchhike, and the two male killers easily found victims who would get into their van for some marijuana or a ride. But when an easier victim could not be found, they would commit every parents' horrifying terror. They would abduct the children. At their worst, these two male killers abducted a young female and tortured her. Sadly, she had been given some bad advice. Someone had told her that if she was ever in sexual danger, she should defecate to scare off the offender. So, she relieved herself in their prized van, and the two men became outraged. This was their prized van that they nicknamed 'Murder Mac.' It was equipped to kill with handcuffs, ice picks, pliers, and anything a sadist would need to have a good time.

For her crime, the two men bound her wrists with rope, and tied the rope to the back of the van. Then they put the van in gear and pulled the frightened young woman by the rope on a stone covered road. Police reported that she did not have one shred of skin on her bloodied body after this brutal attack (Cronin, 1996).

As Lisa recounted dragging Marie behind the car, she appeared to become uncomfortable. I asked Lisa why they didn't just stop killing after they had murdered Marie. Lisa replied:

> We couldn't. At that point in my life, after killing Marie, we couldn't walk away. The rest (of the victims) would've told. Maybe this was something that I really wanted to do. I kind of feel bad that I put this thought in her mind because I knew she'd kill them. We were both at the worst point in our lives, so it wouldn't take much to convince her. It was like, we were both ending our misery. My whole life I wasn't happy with.

Thus, the pair continued their night of mass murder. They had shot and stabbed their victims and actually killed one. But the women kept driving around town deciding who would be next to die.

"So I'm driving like a bat out of hell," said Maddie, "and I turn to Lisa and ask "so what do you want to do?"

"Let's kill them," said Lisa. "Let's kill them all."

Lisa and Maddie said that there was silence in the car after Lisa had said "let's kill them." The victims had heard what she'd said, and they had seen the women kill Marie.

Lisa paused, then described how Carrie was killed. Less than one mile from where they executed Marie, Carrie suffered the same fate. She was ordered out of the car where Lisa pulled her knife out and pressed it against Carrie's neck. She admits to holding it there for a few moments and watching Carrie shake with fear. After a minute, Lisa cut and stabbed Carrie over her chest, back, and under her chin. Like Maire, the knife wounds hadn't killed Carrie, so Maddie shot her in the back of the head. Still, the women weren't finished with their victim yet. Lisa wouldn't talk about this part of the assault, and after Maddie explained what was done, the reason was obvious.

Maddie went on to say "When I was arrested, you know, I had a friend visit me, and she said the sex, you know the gender, of one of the bodies couldn't be determined. You know, something was done to the genitals."

Then they returned to the car where the other three victims waited and proceeded to run over Carrie's body. They sped to the east side of town where they found an empty parking lot in the darkness. Phil, Andy, and Jake sat motionless in the back seat. It was as if prescient evil had left them catatonic and immobile. They were completely paralyzed as if facing a hypnotic vampire.

"So you're telling me that after Marie and Carrie were gone, the others just sat there?" I asked the question with a sense of disbelief. One has to wonder what would make three men sit like they were chained.

Both Maddie and Lisa were surprised by that too. Maddie told an interesting story as to why she thought the men remained:

> Yea, that's true. Not after anyone got killed did the others move. I think they were scared. I was driving around, and I see this alley by this convenience store. In the back was this

parking lot by a field, and I'm sitting there in the parking lot of this closed store. It's dark out, and the man beside me (Phil) is crying. I told him I wasn't going to hurt him, and he said to me if you don't kill me, she will (referring to Lisa). The overhead light was on, and he was leaning over with his hands over his face. He threw up, and I rubbed his back, you know, to soothe him. The next thing I know, Lisa was on him stabbing him repeatedly in the back.

Maddie made a strange comment then, an almost haunting insight to what happened that night. "I remember I laughed."

Lisa stabbed him in the chest five times before she turned him over and stabbed him in the back an additional twelve times. Maddie shot him two times.

One can only recall the words 'batter up' as Lisa and Maddie pulled out their next victim. Andy was pulled out beside Phil's body, where Maddie shot him through each ear. She wouldn't say what that meant or why, but she kept repeating that it felt like a fantasy. Almost simultaneously, Lisa slashed Andy's face, neck, and chest. The knife wounds were described as ugly and ferocious by the medical examiner.

And at this point, it was finally Jake's turn to die. Both women disliked him, and that was why he was forced to watch as his friends were killed. Only after the four had been killed did the women finally turn on Jake. Lisa stabbed him while Maddie shot him.

When asked about his numerous stab wounds, Lisa replied "She (Maddie) had to come get me off of him because I just wanted to keep on and keep on and keep on. I did not like him. I still do not like him. I know there's a reason I feel the way I do towards him. The man is dead. I still shouldn't hate him, but I do."

The hatred literally blazed itself into his body as he suffered the most horrendous of acts, both psychologically and physically. They stabbed him, shot him three times, and ultimately left him for dead. He was alive as they returned to the car and drove away, but the car was stuck on something. So Lisa jumped out of the car and checked underneath the back tire. Maddie followed her and started feeling underneath the tires..

"I felt something cold, like a hand, and it was a foot," said Maddie. She said the feel of cold flesh frightened her, and she started to run away. However, Lisa chased her down. "She was pulling on my shirt, and she said Jake wasn't dead. And she said we had to go back and kill him. I remember going back and holding his head back so Lisa could cut his throat again."

The women returned, picked up Jakes' body, and tossed him back into the car where they set him on fire.

Lisa went on to describe why they set him on fire. "We couldn't take the car, so we caught the car on fire. Then I was going to call a cab and go home."

Amazingly, after being shot, stabbed, and run over, Jake was still alive. Emergency crews responded in time to take Jake to the local hospital where he hovered between life and death.

Lisa laughed and said "That was just the evil coming out in him, is what that was. He was an evil old man. He liked to hit people with his cane, and if I remember right, he had a murder charge against him. I'm not trying to justify why we did what we did. I mean what'd that man ever do to us to deserve that? He didn't deserve that."

"But you said that you still hate him," I interjected.

"I do for some reason," she said.

And in a separate interview, Maddie parroted Lisa. "He was a mean old mother-fucker. He exploited women. He was just nasty, you know? Like he paid the whores to have sex with him and stuff like that. He was a mean mother-fucker."

As my interviews came to a close with Lisa and Maddie, I asked each woman why she killed those five people. Maddie had a very simple answer that she said very matter-of-factly. "I was just pure evil back then."

Lisa, however, was a little unclear as to why she murdered five people. She said:

> When I was stabbing and cutting them, it was like I was releasing all that anger and everything that I had inside of me all the years. After I committed these crimes and went to jail that night, I felt at peace. I slept. I knew then that I didn't have to worry about my clothes. I didn't have to worry about my kids. I didn't have to worry about all that shit no more. That finalized everything because I knew I wasn't going to get out of it. At the trial, I said that I did it because I was afraid of Maddie, but that's a lie. I don't know why I did it. That's not me. If I got out tomorrow, I wouldn't do that again. It's not me. For some reason I needed and wanted to do that, and I did that. But I'm not dangerous. It's not like I'm a dangerous person.

And the interview went silent.

## Control

In order to understand the multiple murderer's mind, a person must learn how to step into the mind of a killer. They see things differently from others, and in order to comprehend why they commit such atrocious acts, a researcher must view where the killer has come from and where the killer is going. This is an example of a how serial killer sees the world based on the experiences and words of the women involved in this research.

You are a young child of five, and you are not like the other children. As you watch them, their heads seem empty to you, those children at preschool. A light seems to surround them as if they were filled with love and joy, and that burns you inside because there is no joy in your life. You don't feel happiness, and no one hugs or kisses you. In fact, mom and dad either left you or they beat you so badly that you wish they had.

As you get older and go to grade school, you find the other kids are different. They seem open and genuinely happy, so you end up alone on the playground, fascinated by thoughts of violence. In your mind, you are omnipotent and all-powerful. No one can hurt you there, so you go into your thoughts all the time. And as you sit quietly on the playground, you learn to *watch* the other children. You learn how their bodies move, and just a few slight movements begin to tell you things. After examining them for a while, you learn who would and who wouldn't fight. It doesn't take long for you to figure out that even the tilt of a head can tell you that someone would be easy to hurt. Then you think about that for a while, fighting with those weaklings just to get that tortured pain out of your mind. You hate them. You hate how they play. You hate the way they laugh and tilt their heads. Nothing makes you happy because you live in despair.

No one really likes you, but then again, you don't have a warm feeling inside like other people. You never did. From the time you were born, there was a cruel emptiness that pretended to protect you. The emptiness kept others away, but nothing ever kept you safe. No one really cared. Oh, how you hate them. As you spend more time alone, you begin to think about actually killing *something*. How would it feel to make something die? Your thoughts are filled with images of knives and blood, and out of the corner of your eyes, you see your mother's cat slinking around the room. That cat. That miserable cat. If you could just take that cat and make him scream, then maybe, you'd feel something.

But what if you got caught? Your parents would make those prior torture sessions seem like a sunny day at the beach. Remember when your foster father sodomized you and poured peroxide into the torn flesh? As the memory skips across your thoughts, a seething hatred rises from your belly. There was nothing you could do when it happened. Nothing at all. You were at the mercy of a vicious monster who seemed to smile as tears crossed your cheeks. Suddenly you notice that your hands have slipped around that cat's throat. He's squirming and clawing at you, but it only makes you squeeze harder. Your icy eyes scan his twitching body as his eyes look directly into yours. He almost seems to be asking "why?" And you notice the corners of your mouth rising in a salute to his pain. Then, almost in a slow-motion minute, there is nothing. He stops moving, and you look at this rag doll that is clutched in your hands. He's quiet now, and you feel so good. You did it, and it felt right. As if to toss a crumpled piece of paper into the garbage, you drop his listless corpse to the floor.

Mother will be home soon, but suddenly, you're not so afraid anymore. You feel something new now, something different. And you start to wonder what your mother's face will look like when she sees her precious little kitty lying on top of the garbage cans. You take the body and toss it outside with a glee that fills every muscle in your body. You wait. You listen. And when she comes home, she finds kitty with flies circling his head. Mom looks different, almost fearful. Did I do that, you ask. Could I have scared her? The one who beat me and locked me in the closet?

You notice that something has changed. "What happened to kitty?" she asks in a controlled tone. But you notice her eyes are different. They used to be filled with assurance, so full of self-confidence. Now there's a question in her eyes, and the question is you. You're still a little frightened of what she will do. She's bigger than you. So you qui-

etly say that you don't know what happened to kitty. She doesn't believe you, you can see it in those questioning eyes. Yet she doesn't do
anything. Maybe it's that question running through her head. Perhaps
she knows something now that she didn't before. Again, the corners of
your mouth rise. You can't help it. You've just learned something that
you'll never forget. And suddenly, your world becomes an abyss.

Time goes by, and you find that you're a teenager. You run away to
hide from the terrible people in your life, but you always have to come
back since you have no money. And they make you go back to school.
Those teenagers who date now, you wish them pain and suffering, just
like you have suffered. They ignore you though you are in plain sight,
making you feel like nothing. It hurts to feel like a nobody. But then
again, they are the true nobodies. They are nothing. Those kids at
school, the parents that you never had, they are all nothings just like
the cat that you held in your hands. Perhaps doing something to another person would make you feel better. After all, those thoughts that
you have, those wicked pictures of wrapping your fingers around another person's throat are dominating your life now. You can't think of
much else, and you even begin to learn about police and how they in-
vestigate homicides.

Is it curiosity? Is it planning? In your own head, it's merely a way
to be more powerful. The more you know, the more you can do. And
when you think about killing, you want to do more. Take yourself further into the darkness and begin to think like a serial murderer. Those
warm holidays filled with a family that loved you: they do not exist.
They never did. The warmth you share with your spouse or lover must
be annihilated. Feel nothing. Be nothing. Hate. Revenge. Indignity.
Separate yourself away from your heart. Recall the loneliest time in
your life. Remember when your dreams died? How bad was the pain
when that one person you loved abandoned you? Do you stay awake at

night, tears streaming down your face because no will help you? Let it envelop you, taking you whole. Turn the pain outside of yourself. After all, you have to survive, and only the strongest pull ahead. The others, they just get in your way, and all the while they smile with their spar-kling eyes as you wither away into a hole of the unknown. If you could strike at them, or maybe, if you could strike at someone else. . .

When you take yourself apart into this nothingness, sit and think quietly about all of those nothings who smile and laugh around you, right in front of you. They can see your pain, yet they smile and go on with their happiness. You are left behind, and they move by you like *you* are a nothing. Imagine, those creatures of nothingness, mocking you. Just what is it that drives your thoughts now? Is it a need to fit in? No, remember, people do not exist as loved ones to you. They are nothings to be maligned. Pause once more, and remember, you have no heart. Do you want to be a giver, one who makes others better for the world? You should laugh at that question, for compassion and empathy do not exist in your world. You are within yourself a complete mass of unwanted fury, and surely, fury wishes no one well. So there is no love, and there is no joy. Life means little to you, doesn't it?

Everything and everyone is reduced to a fleck of dust, and you find yourself beginning to want to act out. What is it that you want to do to them? What would make you feel better? What would make you feel anything? Slowly, the word will creep into your consciousness like the answer to your darkened prayers. Control. There is nothing in your world but an emptiness and the repetitive thought that if only others could feel the pain that you've endured, then maybe, you will 'feel.' There must be something to this 'feeling,' why else would it make those nothings happy? Remember, people are nothing in your world but a means to an end, and to be an instrument, a person must be controlled. An instrument is inanimate, a nothing.

In following the above thought pattern, you enter the beginning stages of the multiple murderer's mind where people are hated, joy is reviled, and love is a four-letter word.

## Domination

It's all about control, for both serial and mass murderers. They don't have it. They want it. Certain types of male serial killers clearly demonstrate a desperate need to dominate their victims. Often, they are anal personality types who do things the same way repeatedly. This compulsion to control emerges in their everyday lives. They will fre-quently have clothing arranged neatly in their closets, and nothing can be moved from its prearranged position. Similarly, one accused serial killer was known to follow his wife around the house as she vacuumed so that he could "rub out" the tracks caused by the wheels (San Fran-cisco Chronicle, Allen Matthews Thursday July 20, 1995).

Another control fanatic was convicted serial killer Gerald Gallego who participated in the murders of four young women along with his common-law wife Charlene Gallego. The Gallego couple was quite unique in their quest for blood and murder. In fact, Gerald Gallego was the epitome of a control freak, using his domination over Charlene to force her into securing victims for rape and murder. But using the woman for bait (remember, she is a nothing instrument) was not all that Gerald demanded. In what is perhaps the most peculiar and bla-tant example of exerting control over another human being, Gerald Gallego made Charlene look and dress like a prepubescent girl, and he even required that she call him 'daddy.' (Von Hoffman, 1990).

Females are no exception to the rule, for they crave that drug of domination as much as any male. What is similar is the deep seeded desire to have control. It was obvious when I interviewed female serial and mass murderers how important the issue of control was to these women. It pervaded the interviews in some form or another, and they tried to get it whenever they could. Every killer that I interviewed lacked power while she was growing up, and killing served to restore a sense of well-being. In other words, female multiple murderers are remarkable in their search for a sense of being in control.

Many of the women I interviewed had read about mass and serial murder and knew some of what I was studying. Like males, they educate themselves about crime scene investigation and autopsy procedures. They had read about male multiple murderers, and knew about the common factors in male backgrounds. One frequent behavior pattern seen in the lives of male multiple murderers is cruelty to animals and other children. So when I asked the women in my study about their relationship with animals, they knew what I was asking about.

However, there were those profile questions that they just could not figure out, and that drove some of these ladies mad. Profiling questions are designed to seek characteristics that can be used to pinpoint the type of person who commits certain types of crimes. A profiler wants to know about what a killer looked like at the time of the murder, what type of car that person drives, where the person lives, and things like that.

One woman in particular was brash, one of the most overt psychopaths I had ever met. She had killed three men and two women and had tried to kill nine others. She was intelligent (as were most of the women I interviewed). She had dropped out of high school, yet she was street smart. She sensed that I didn't like being touched, so she purposely kept reaching across the table grab at my arms and hands. It was hard pretending that I didn't mind, but she knew. This woman wanted control. She tried to dominate questions and conversation from the minute I was locked into the room with her. But I started asking her about the color of her car. I asked if she rented a house or an apartment. Did she wear slacks or jeans? As the barrage of profiling questions hit her, she quickly became agitated. Her face, which had been like an inanimate doll, suddenly turned and appeared distorted. She actually started breathing faster. Her hands fidgeted on the table. She was *physically* angered as she began to realize that she was not in control of the interview.

"I don't understand why you're asking this. What are you getting at?"

That flat face became flushed, she grit her teeth, and she pounded on the table with her closed fists. She was well versed in serial and mass murder, and accordingly, she knew a lot of the questions before I asked them. However since she had not been trained in profiling, she didn't know what the 'acceptable' answers were for those questions. In other words, she knew male serial killers had come from violent homes, enjoyed a sick fantasy life, and stalked their victims. So she knew that she was going to be asked about those things. Unfortunately for her, it is much harder to figure out what a profiler is looking for in an interview. Just when you think we're getting at one topic, we really are getting at another that you hadn't thought about. She answered my questions, but it really aggravated her not to know what I was looking for. And as anyone can see, her first response to frustration was violence.

**The Sadist**

In its most simplistic form, sadism involves sexual gratification from inflicting punishment on another person (Holmes, 1991). The sadist likes to make other people suffer, and the more the person suffers, the better the sadist feels. From an early age, the sadist pairs inflicting violence with his own sexual stimulation (Holmes, 1996). In other words, the more pain the sadist can inflict on someone, the more it turns him on. Sadistic sex is common among male serial killers. Most serial murder involving male offenders revolves around some twisted sexual torment. For instance, recall the two sexual predators who tortured young women who got into their precious van. Their acts are among the most heinous in history.

The female multiple murderer, like the male, craves domination, and the female has even been known to sexually ravage a helpless victim as well. The sadistic female killer who I interviewed came across as charming, but then again, that is the hallmark of the serial killer. She had short brown hair and light green eyes that seemed to dance as she spoke. She had killed heterosexual males and heterosexual females.

> I would use handcuffs or chains so I could have more control or dominate them (victims) more. I didn't know any other way, and I thought everybody liked it that way. In fact I'm going to tell you something. When I first got into prostitution and started turning tricks, men would ask me to beat them. One man said I'll give you five hundred dollars for you to beat me with this whip. I said no, I'm not going to beat you. Then I thought, for five hundred dollars, I could beat you to death, and I did. I got mad at him and got carried away. And I liked it because it let me have *control*, you know what I'm saying. And that's just the way that I like it. Like before I was in here (prison), if I was having sex with a trick or someone who wasn't into it (sadism), I'd have to be in control in other ways, like being on top. I may not have gotten violent with them because there were people I couldn't *control*, you know what I'm saying? I liked hurting people. It's like an animal instinct in me.

This convicted multiple murderer described making another woman bleed during violent sex by inserting a foreign object violently into her vagina:

> It (the weapon) was a pipe. See what happens is I get a little carried away. I don't know why I do this. It seems like *the more it hurts the other person, the better I like it.* She (the victim) had had a hysterectomy, and I made her bleed real bad. She should've never been bleeding. (Author's files).

This sadistic killer was adamantly turned on by violent pornography, which she was introduced to at age 16 by a boyfriend. In fact, she never was excited by 'normal' pornography that did not involve violence. She said she wanted something that was more exciting than 'normal' sex. So, she sought out violent videos that she would watch by herself, and she would attend peep shows to feed her sexual cravings. To her, sex without inflicting pain was boring. She went on to say:

> It was like a fantasy really. Subconsciously I wanted to do that for a long time (hurt people). I would fantasize about hurting people, bringing blood to someone, you know just hurting someone. *I just wanted to hear somebody scream.* The louder the better. I'm telling you when I first started doing this, I didn't see anything wrong with it. I've always wanted to bite off someone's nipple and taste flesh. That's just something I've always wanted to do just to see what it felt like. I mean I wanted to do this ever since I was little. I wanted to bite off someone's flesh. (Author's files).

And yet another serial killer who admits to murdering six people said that she liked having power over people as well. She enjoyed having control over life and death and laughed as she said:

> It's terrible and its bad to say, but it was like hey, I can do something you can't do. And that's where all my troubles

started. In my mind, I was doing something other people couldn't do and get away with it. Here all these police and doctors were like, they didn't know what was going on. These people should know homicide when they see it, but they didn't.

Surely, this is one of the most clearly stated control motivations. She even said the word over and over to make sure I understood what she was saying. The theme of control ran throughout the interviews like a warm knife through butter. Within their lives, they had felt powerless against a parade of horrible events, and in order for them to restore a sense of balance (at least in their minds), they used the murders of other people like many people use a cigarette. Think of all people who crowd outside for that cigarette break from work. They crave it because it calms them down, for within it, though they know it is bad for them, it serves as an immediate source of pleasure. And to the female multiple murderer, controlling another human being to death serves the same purpose. They are seeking a calm in their lives that they will never have, and deep down, they truly know it will never 'fix' their lives.

Killing is all about control and all of the feelings that come with it. By committing murder, female multiple killers hoped to create a sense of power and control which they never had in their lives. This is largely what drives them to commit their crimes. Whatever their method of killing, and of those interviewed, the methods included death by knife, gun, poison, strangulation, suffocation, lethal injection, and even fire, the deep-seated desire to be all-powerful was ever-present. The words were similar from interview to interview, and they must not be ignored.

# 7

## BEHAVIOR PATTERNS

## Behavioral Indicators

Before someone can appreciate the mindset of those who commit acts of multiple murder, it is essential to glean those factors which act on a continuum throughout that individual's life. What cues or behavioral warning signals are present during the formative years, when an offender moves from childhood to adolescence? In most instances, there are concrete examples of deviant behavior, which span back into early childhood. Those actions are often overt but are ignored by caretakers who are clueless as to the meaning behind the behaviors.

## Cruelty To Animals

It is well known that acts of violence directed at small animals are indicators of potential future violence against human beings. Studies have consistently demonstrated that male multiple murderers engaged in some type of animal cruelty in early childhood and adolescence (Ressler, et al., 1988). Most often, the deviant behavior is directed at cats, as they are easy targets and their absence is not as quickly noticed as dogs'. Aggressive acts, research indicates, include skinning, cutting, and even setting fire to these small creatures in order to make the animals suffer.

This research confirmed the hypothesis that females who proceed to acts of multiple murder engaged in similar antisocial behaviors against small animals. Again, it is important to note that a predatory pattern is established early in life. All seven women involved in this research demonstrated a history of violence with small animals that was noted, but ignored. This violence began as early as age seven, and like their male counterparts, the females chose cats as the primary targets of their predation. In fact, in the interviews, six women reported killing at least one cat before age ten. The women admitted to hunting the small animals after encountering a stressful situation within the home.

Apparently, there was a common trigger that started the deviant behavior. Each woman noted that the killing began after a parental figure had abused her. Most often, the abuse was emotional. Cruel words and/or fights fueled the episodes. After suffering some type of verbal humiliation at the hands of a caregiver, the females would launch out in search of something they could injure. There was a stated preference for cats, although at least three women admitted to killing whatever little animal they could catch — small dogs or even rabbits from the neighbor's hutches. Interestingly, there was a preferred method of murder when killing small animals as well: asphyxia. Two women reported hanging cats, one drowned them, two strangled cats, and one woman reported eviscerating a cat with a penknife. The remaining woman recalled torturing her mother's dog by beating it to death with rocks. The dog was a small terrier, and the female mass murderer laughed as she recalled the actual torture that preceded the animal's death:

> I hated that dog shit. I wanted him dead, and I knew she (her
> mother) loved him. She'd make all over him like this (acts

out hugging and kissing). Like he was some precious little piece of shit. I hated that little shit (pauses and laughs). But she couldn't love him no more because after I got a hold of him, he was as good as dead. I was sitting in the living room, and she was at the store. The little shit was yipping at me, like a little son of a bitch. And that sound was in my ears. Yip. Yip. Yip. I couldn't take it no more. I grabbed that little shit by his neck and took him out back in the woods. See, there were these trees in back of the house. No one could see what I was doing. I always made sure there weren't no one to see what I was doing. And I took the clothesline and tied his back legs together so he there wasn't nowhere he could go. I picked up a stick and whacked him upside his head, and finally that little shit quit yipping at me. I liked that he stopped yipping, and I kept hitting him with sticks and rocks until he *cried*. Yea, it was like he was this crying little baby, and the more he cried, the more I liked it. It was like hey, finally (makes huge gesture with arms), something else feels like I do. Let something else suffer for a change. He wasn't getting it any worse than I got it, and he was just a dog. I was like throwing and throwing things at him, and there was, you know, blood everywhere. It was like, hey, finally I'm in charge. I'm the judge, and I can make him cry. And I thought, *I can make him die*. I can kill him, and I wanted to see what would happen if I killed him. So I kept throwing things at him until he didn't get up no more. I buried him in the woods under this big tree that fell. You couldn't see it, so no one was going to find it. And I went back inside and washed my hands and stuff, and by the time she got home, he was gone. She *cried* after that. I was like, hey, I haven't seen him, but she knew it. But there wasn't nothing she could do about it.

It should be noted that this same killer murdered five children who were in her care. She stated that their crying upset her, and the noise triggered her acts of violence.

Another female recalls stringing up the neighborhood cats in her barn, with rope. She was only nine years old when she began acting out against small animals, but the memories are vivid to the offender. One by one, she would stalk and catch neighborhood felines and hang them behind the cars in her parents' barn. Her recollection was clear, not only of attacking the cats, but of being caught as well. "She (stepmother) came right to me and my brother. Now, she knew it was me, but I never admitted to it. That would be stupid. But she knew I'd done it, and that's what it took for her to beat me with her shoe. At least that time I deserved it."

This convicted killer stated that the acts of violence directed towards the cats were actual attempts to hurt her foster mother. In other words, the small animals acted as a receptacle for the anger directed at a parental figure. This female killer felt as if the animals received love that she did not, and in order to inflict pain upon the foster mother, she killed the cats. She noted that this caused the foster mother great pain, and she enjoyed watching the woman suffer. In one instance, she hanged three cats by the neck with chicken wire and left them in plain view for her foster mother to find. The feeling of inflicting pain on both the cats as well as her foster mother was that of elation. As the woman described it, "It was like getting high."

When asked how she felt when she committed violence against an animate being, she was callous and displayed no empathy.

"You're acting like it mattered to me," she said.

This author pressed the woman and again asked what she felt when she killed the animals. The question seemed to frustrate her.

> The only way I could answer your question would be to lie because I didn't feel anything. I know how that sounds. But you need to listen to what I am saying. I never feel much of anything. I didn't when I hung the cats, and I didn't when I stabbed those people. I knew I'd be taken care of, no matter what I did. What's anybody going to do to me? Kill me?"

This offender was asked to clarify what she meant. Her response was interesting.

> I've been dead since I was five. I stopped feeling cause all I knew was hurt. And I got so damned tired of hurting. I made it so I couldn't hurt anymore, and when you stop feeling, you stop living. I was dead, (says interviewer's name). I am dead. So what's prison going to do to me? Lock me up? Kill me? You can't kill me, 'cause I'm dead. You can't kill a corpse. I'm here, and I knew they'd (the prison) take care of me. It's better in here than out there. (Expletive), I don't have to do nothing in here. They feed me. They keep it warm. You think this is worse than I had it? (Expletive), it's better in here.

Yet another commonality was discovered in this research: victim selection. Females prey upon cats because they are easy to catch and typically could not injure the women. It was important to the females not to be hurt in the process of killing; so, they chose animals small enough that they could control. When asked why they did not kill dogs, the typical response was that dogs were too big and could bite them. Cats were small and often unable to scratch or bite, thus leaving the women without any injuries. This is significant, as female multiple killers choose extremely helpless victims who cannot injure them. Thus, the pattern of victim selection is also established early in life.

It is clear that female multiple murderers engage in patterns of predatory behavior beginning in the formative years. The violence is most commonly directed at small animals, cats being the victim of choice. There is a sequence of events preceding the violence that each female acknowledged. The offenses began after the females suffered from some form of emotional abuse perpetrated by a caregiver. The abuse created feelings of anger and isolation that led the females to predate on small animals. The preferred method of killing was asphyxia, though several women admitted to torturing the cats before strangling them. Furthermore, it appears as if the acts of killing were not merely directed at the felines. Specifically, the animals acted as forms of displacement for intense feelings of anger. Since the women could not act out against those individuals who were creating the stress, they instead focused on objects (animals) that they could easily acquire with minimal risk to their safety.

### Verbal Skills

Though inconclusive, many studies point to the fact that male multiple killers have difficulty expressing themselves verbally. Whether they stutter or simply suffer from an inability to use the correct words, many male killers have a hard time speaking and writing (Cronin, 1996). This difficulty in communicating thoughts and ideas further separates the multiple murderers from mainstream society. The lack of verbal skills serves to isolate these killers once again, and this reinforces, to the killers, the notion that they are different from others. Once more, anger increases as does aggression.

What was remarkable about the female offenders involved in this research was that they clearly suffered from verbal difficulties. They remarked that they experienced great difficulty communicating with both adults and other children while growing up. Six of the women stated that they could not verbalize their thoughts and feelings when they were young. The primary reason given was an inability to articulate what they meant; they could not find the appropriate words to express themselves, and they also reported that this inability to articulate their feelings caused significant emotional distress. The women were also unable to express themselves in writing. Again, the chief complaint was the inability to find the appropriate words to communicate their thoughts. Much like male offenders, this leads to increased levels of isolation and anger, which in turn becomes suppressed aggression.

Even though they did find it troublesome to write, the women acknowledged keeping diaries of their day-to-day activities, which included their plans of murder. When asked how they could keep a detailed record when they could not successfully verbalize, they each suggested that it was easier to write out a murder plan than their feelings. It was simple to articulate a methodical sequence that involved step-by-step instructions for killing someone as opposed to writing about how they *felt* about doing those acts. Thus, it would appear that the obstacle to verbalization involves recognizing and expressing feelings, rather than everyday terms.

It may be suggested that the females have trouble communicating their feelings because they were never allowed to express emotion. Bowlby (1944) points out that children who are separated from a primary caregiver for lengths of time eventually have trouble recognizing their feelings, because they become detached from their primary caregiver. This detachment seems to translate into other relationships and thus other parts of a child's life. In other words, when a child isolates himself from others, he must shut down emotionally. This would describe why multiple murderers have difficulty recognizing and expressing themselves (their emotions).

When examining the backgrounds of females who commit multicide, or on the other hand, children who are exhibiting questionable behaviors, it may be wise to examine whether those children have trouble expressing their emotions, both written and verbal. It would be beneficial to question teachers and family to determine how much difficulty the child has in expressing his or her feelings. Often, teachers will note a "blackout" in the speech patterns of such children. For example, a child will not be able to answer simple question such as "how are you feeling today?" Instead of answering, the child will simply discuss some other topic, typically one that does not involve emotion. Those children who suffer from this difficulty should be examined more closely for the other significant warning signs present in this research. These signals should never be ignored, as they could be predictors of future violence.

**Sleep Dysfunction**

Sleep deprivation is common among male multiple murderers (Ressler, et al., 1988). As children and as adults, these offenders suffer from nightmares, night terrors, and even sleep walking which prevent these individuals from obtaining significant periods of rest. Sleepwalking occurs when an individual rises and walks while asleep. Nightmares are frightening cognitions that occur during rest periods. Finally, when an individual thrashes around in bed and wakes up in a panic or screaming, this is a night terror.

A similar pattern emerged upon asking females about their sleep patterns, but there was one twist. Not only do females suffer from sleep dysfunction, but they also tend to dislike the nighttime. For female predators, the inability to sleep is terrifying. All seven women reported excessive disturbances in their slumber patterns that included sleepwalking, night terrors and nightmares. These disturbances precluded the subjects from acquiring minimal levels of slumber, which in turn contributed to high levels of stress. As previously mentioned, multiple murderers in general are not adept at handling acute or longitudinal stressors.

All seven women acknowledge erratic sleep patterns and a preference for daytime rest. Furthermore, most of the women stated that they "feared" the night because of these sleep disturbances. Because of this fear, the women had a habit of roaming the house at night in order to avoid trying to sleep. Being nocturnal was their way of coping with a phobia of sleeping at night. The nighttime wanderings were well-known in the households where the women resided; almost all members of the house knew of their sleep disorders. However, even though there was an awareness regarding the sleep situations, there was no intervention. This was true even when the women were children. Their problems were ignored, and no treatment was sought. Again, this is another pattern that is remarkable.

When they did sleep, it was common for the women to engage in sleepwalking. They recalled waking up while moving about in some part of their homes. Typically, they became confused upon awakening and returned to their beds. However, as a result of the sleepwalking, the women became highly stressed and concerned for their safety. In fact, of those who engaged in sleepwalking, all stated that they were hurt while doing it. Injuries included cuts, contusions, and abrasions caused by bumping into or running into objects in the dark. One case was very severe. A female serial killer recounts the incident as follows:

> I went to bed around ten, which was past my bedtime. Uh, we'd (she and her mother) fight back and forth. You know what I'm saying? And, uh, she'd say go (to bed), and I'd say there wasn't any way I was going to bed. And she'd take her shoe or beer bottle or you know, what was laying there. And she'd whack me in the head until I was about beat to death. And I'd, uh, go to bed and lay there and lay there and wait until I was sure she was asleep. And I'd, uh, go down the hall and, uh, down the stairs and in the kitchen and back up-stairs and back in bed. One time, I woke up downstairs. I remember feeling a pain in my right arm. Blood all over it (motions from elbow to wrist), and I saw the door and was like oh. Oh shit. And I knew what I'd done (in her sleep, she ran into the sliding glass door and punctured her right arm on a nail that protruded from the frame). All I could think of was cleaning it up before she heard anything. You know what I'm saying? I'd been beat up enough that night, and I didn't want no more.

Similarly, almost all of the female multiple killers remembered having terrible nightmares involving violence and abandonment. Each woman recalled being repeatedly chased by several people in their nightmares, which occurred on a regular basis. This caused an intense level of fear, which always resulted in the young female waking up shaking and with rapid heartbeat. They have distinct recollections concerning repetitive dreams about being left alone. One woman who was convicted of five homicides had a recurring nightmare that involved her family floating away from her on an iceberg. No matter what she did to get their attention, there was nothing that would make her family return to her, so she was left alone.

The nightmares centered on being chased or being abandoned, and as the research demonstrated, female multiple murderers come from homes where they are physically abused (often chased) as well as abandoned. Therefore, it is not surprising that their nightmares would focus on the ills in their lives. It is noteworthy that each woman had vivid recollections regarding her nightmares. When asked why she could remember her dreams so completely, each woman responded the same way. All of these women suffered from intense nightmares in childhood and in adolescence. For some women, the nightmares continue, and that explains why there is great detail recall. The dreams were repetitive and longitudinal. Table 6-7 summarizes sleep disturbances.

### Adolescent Behaviors

Adolescence was a critical point in the lives of multiple murderers. For male offenders, it was common to engage in antisocial activities such as running away, lying, and criminal activities. For the females, there were high levels of deviance as well. Almost all of the women were chronic runaways beginning in early adolescence. The reasons for running away ranged from "needing a break from getting beat up," to "I wanted to die." This latter mass murderer admits to running away and

| Table 6-7 summarizes sleep disturbances | | |
|---|---|---|
| Characteristic | Number/Total | Percent |
| Sleep Disturbances | 7/7 | 100 |
| Preference for Daytime Sleep | 7/7 | 100 |
| Sleep Phobia | 6/7 | 86.0 |
| Sleep Avoidance | 5/7 | 71.0 |
| Sleepwalking | 5/7 | 71.0 |
| Injuries Caused by Sleepwalking | 5/7 | 71.0 |
| Nightmares | 5/7 | 71.0 |
| Night Terrors | 4/7 | 57.0 |

hitchhiking in an area where a male serial killer was picking up prostitutes who resembled her. "In a way, I wanted to die because I heard about the maniac and what he was doing." This female was picked up by a violent man who pulled a gun on her and raped her in his car.

> After he was finished, you know, when he came [ejaculated], he threw me out the side door on the grass. I could barely see because he hit me across my eyes with the gun. I thought I was going to die, and why he didn't shoot me, I don't know. Since I was a whore, I knew enough to shut up when he pulled the gun. You don't [expletive] with people like that.

This female continued to hitchhike her way back home, though she knew she could be picked up by a killer.

Another female serial killer admitted to running away to see how far she could get before her mother would find her. She enjoyed playing cat and mouse with her mother, knowing in the end she would always return home.

It appears as if the act of running away was not so much for enjoyment as much as an escape for the young women. In other words, they were retreating from a bad situation by leaving, if only temporarily. The act was often not meant to punish caregivers as much as it was to soothe high anxiety levels. Again, like most antisocial activity, there was a definite trigger that set them off before the women ran away. Most often, the trigger was a mixture of physical and emotional abuse, which was so severe as to make the women physically run. Most of the women had been raped and beaten, and as they grew older, they no longer merely sought escape in their thoughts. Instead they took to physical flight to avoid the pain.

Truancy from school was a common trait as well. All the women admitted to disliking the educational process, and all received average to poor grades while in school. It was not uncommon for the females to ignore homework assignments and miss class. They had no friends or social activities associated with education, and they hated learning. Thus, lack of effort and interest were instrumental in the decision to skip school. When asked why they did not enjoy education, the women stated that there was no clear benefit to being there. One serial killer summed up the attitude:

> I didn't want to be there, so I was a terror. I wasn't paying attention to nobody, and they didn't pay attention to me. What was I gonna be, anyway? It wasn't like there was something for me later in life. I was finished before I got started, so it wasn't like I had a future. There was nothing for me, at school. So why go?

Apparently, a decision had been made early in life that served to direct future decisions. That is, the women decided when they were young that they had no future for which to strive. They did not feel as if attending school would make their lives better because they had no positive examples or role models to emulate. Everywhere they looked, women were caregivers who were mistreated. Happiness was nonexistent. Accordingly, there was nothing to hope for. They viewed education as a hindrance and another unpleasant experience. Therefore, they avoided it, much as they avoided the bad situations at home by running away. This demonstrates a pattern of escapism developing early in childhood.

In yet another escapist activity, the women were hooked on cigarettes and drinking at a young age. Most times, introduction to these bad habits was made by a caregiver, usually the mother. No sanctions resulted when they did engage in smoking and drinking, so habits were formed. They enjoyed having sex with older men. The women admitted to a first consensual intercourse before age 14. Remarkably, their sex partners were typically in their early 20's as opposed to someone their own age. They viewed the older men as an escape (they used that word). They believed in a fairytale-like fantasy in which a prince rescues a threatened woman. The women viewed the older men as possible escapes from their horrible lives, in essence, the princes to come rescue them. Why? Older men tended to have monetary resources, which were attractive to the young women. Remember that the socioeconomic status in the females' homes was poor.

One serial killer reported her first sexual relations with a man in his 60's. He was a school bus driver, and as the serial killer recalled, the driver was "the only man who ever asked me out." They had sex on the first date, which was conducted in secret. "My mother would have freaked out," said the convicted killer. "I said I was going to a friend's house, but I met Butch and ended up having sex in his car. I was on the rag at the time, but he didn't seem to care. So we did it in his back seat. It wasn't the best thing, but hell, it was better than getting my ass kicked at home."

Because they engaged in promiscuous sexual behavior, six women got pregnant before age 18. This is pivotal, as all of the women had a strong desire to have children. However, though they wanted the children, when they did give birth, they did not want to care for the kids — they had not realized how difficult it is to raise a child. Most gave up

131

their babies. Apparently, it was the idea of having a child rather than the reality of the situation that appealed to the female offenders. One mass murderer stated:

> I always wanted kids. Cause like, they were, uh, to me, it was like a dream. Kids, uh, to me, it was like they, uh, kids would love me um, like somehow or, it was like, um, that's what was missing. When I, uh, Katie was born and I, um, I was seventeen. It, uh, having a kid isn't like that. Um, cause like, you gotta be a, you know, looking after her, um, it's like, that's not, it wasn't what I thought. I mean, it's like, when you're, um, when you, uh, get like a present but it's, um, like it wasn't what you wanted. That was Katie. Um, I didn't want her.

Despite this intense desire to have children, almost all of the women acknowledged at least one abortion in their teens. The reasons ranged from "I wasn't ready yet," to "I wasn't gonna have his kid." There was no cognitive dissonance related to aborting the baby. The act was viewed as a means to an end. Though having a family was important, giving birth (usually after already having and giving up a child) was not an option.

## Predation

A lion stalks a gazelle on the plains. A cat follows a bird near a feeder. These are inherent actions pre-programmed in predator behavior. Female multiple killers begin predatory actions at a young age. In fact, several women reported molesting a playmate or neighbor sexually. The abuse of others started when the young female entered adolescence. Preferred targets were other females of the same age or younger, and the assaults occurred at approximately the age of 12. However, no criminal charges were brought against any of the young females in this study. One female mass murderer convicted of five murders recalled one of these events vividly:

> We were in the bathroom (at school), and I kind of brought her (a friend) into the stall where we-I took her pants off. It's kind of like a dream really. I see these visions like it didn't but did happen, you know? I put her in, I mean we were in the stall, and I was licking her. But she wasn't screaming or nothing. I mean I wasn't hurting her or nothing like that. She didn't say nothing, so it was okay. I mean it wasn't like she was screaming or nothing. You hear what I'm saying? Are you understanding what I'm saying. She wasn't screaming. It wasn't like I was beating her or nothing like that. She wasn't in no pain, you know? It wasn't until after we were through she was crying, and she wouldn't come near me after that.

When asked whether she coerced her friend into the bathroom stall, this convicted murderer said that she could not remember. That part of the incident, according the female killer, is blacked out. However, she did admit to removing the young female's clothing and performing oral sex on the girl. This killer was asked if she would have ceased the activity if the girl had screamed, and the reply was odd. "But she wasn't screaming," said the mass murderer. "I already told you that. She wasn't in no pain." Strangely, this killer recognized the crying reaction as one of displeasure and admitted that the girl did not want to engage in sex activities. In other words, this female mass murderer acknowledged that this act was nonconsensual. However her reaction was one of indifference to the crying of the young girl.

There was no sympathy for the victim in each case. The women viewed their predatory acts as "experimentation," not something bad. Despite forcing themselves on other children, their strongly held beliefs were that the acts were natural, and they had done nothing wrong. One will find this mindset as the female multiple killer proceeds through life.

## Stop, Thief!

Another striking result of this research is the incidence of petty theft. In addition to running away, lying, killing small animals and preying on other children, almost all of the seven convicted multiple murderers admitted to stealing. The thefts occurred during adolescence, and the targets were primarily retail stores. However, three females admitted to stealing from both stores and family. Items stolen included money (6/7), clothing (5/7), and makeup (3/7). When asked why they stole these items, the primary response was lack of money (6/7) followed by "to hurt someone else" (5/7). The thefts appear to be a continual behavior pattern, which extended into adulthood. Another notable commonality: no remorse. Not one women felt bad about her actions. Like the other activities, it was viewed as a means to an end.

Table 6-8 summarizes adolescent performance characteristics.

| Table 6-8 Adolescent Characteristics | | |
|---|---|---|
| **Characteristic** | **Number/Total** | **Percent** |
| Running Away | 6/7 | 86.0 |
| First Consensual Sex before 14 | 6/7 | 86.0 |
| Early Pregnancy (before age 18) | 6/7 | 86.0 |
| Truancy | 5/7 | 71.0 |
| Smoking | 5/7 | 71.0 |
| Drinking Alcohol | 5/7 | 71.0 |
| Sex with Men at Least 10 Years Older | 5/7 | 71.0 |
| Abortion | 4/7 | 57.0 |
| Molesting Other Children | 4/7 | 57.0 |
| Miscarriage | 2/7 | 29.0 |

**Education**

Only three of the seven women finished high school; four dropped out. The general attitude about school was a critical one — as previously mentioned, the women hated school. Because they felt like outsiders, six considered school a miserable place. There were general feelings of discomfort and an inability to fit in. This led to increased levels of isolation and eventually truancy. Six of the seven sat in the back of the classroom because they wanted to be ignored. Generally, the females involved in this research were poor students. In fact, only two received any above-average grades. There was no participation in class discussions, and there were no attempts to participate in small groups.

Below is a table that presents enduring characteristics associated with female multicide. Note the high levels of depression, attention to appearance, lack of formal education, and deviant behaviors.

There were, however, indications that the female multiple murderer is a creative being. Six of seven engaged in writing or drawing as teenagers. These creative projects proved to be outlets for inner frustrations. Drawings consisted of overly perfect landscapes and homes, but writings entailed mainly violent and dark images. The writings and drawings were personal in nature and only kept by the offender. In fact,

| Table 6-9 Enduring Psychological Characteristics | | |
|---|---|---|
| **Characteristic** | **Number/Total** | **Percent** |
| Depression | 6/7 | 87.0 |
| Fantasy | 6/7 | 87.0 |
| Theft | 6/7 | 87.0 |
| Attention to Appearance | 5/7 | 71.0 |
| Self Education about Murder | 5/7 | 71.0 |
| High School Drop-Out | 4/7 | 57.0 |
| Children | 4/7 | 57.0 |
| Abandoned Their Children | 3/7 | 75.0 |
| Legally Employed | 4/7 | 57.0 |

all women kept these works and still have them to this day. They admit that they never showed them to anyone, for fear of being ridiculed.

It is clear that behavioral patterns are clearly established in the lives of female multiple killers. From thievery to predatory actions, there are neon-warning signs which if educated, a person could plainly recognize. Having difficulty verbalizing and learning makes the female prone to feeling more vulnerable and therefore likely to run away. She doesn't sleep well, suffers from nightmares, and sleepwalks. Being so frustrated and angry, the female turns to acts of deviancy to escape the pain, but she goes too far and begins hurting animals and then humans. The cycle begins early, and if not stopped, will eventually turn into homicide.

# 8
## PROFILING

## Overview

*The Silence of the Lambs.*
*Profiler.*
*Millennium.*

These movies and television shows have captivated the American public. Society has been fascinated by the notion that an expert, a profiler, could understand a serial predator. Twisted thoughts and actions. Who could fathom such horrific things? Being one of those experts, a profiler, this author can attest to the fact that profiling violent crimes and their perpetrators is not an easy task. It takes years of study and an intense memory to turn what has been sometimes been described as "smoke and mirrors" into a tangible investigative tool.

Many times over, I have been approached by police officers and students who want to know what it takes to become a respected profiler. The answer is always the same. It is essential to comprehend the background of an individual in order to understand how that person thinks and behaves. Whether examining someone suffering from depression, anxiety, or even someone who commits multiple murder, in order to appreciate that person's world view, one must look at how that individual has responded (and what that person has been subjected to) in the past. It has been said that the best predictor for future behavior is past behavior, and this is why good profilers study the lives of multiple murderers before actually becoming profilers. Knowing how an individual sees himself and others can narrow the list of possible characteristics that can be seen when dealing with a multiple killer. In other words, research has shown that certain types of people engage in specific behaviors when they offend. For example, if a profiler knows that an offender is likely to be an introvert with a history of stuttering or verbalizing problems, it is highly unlikely that such an individual would approach a victim in a public place where he would risk scrutiny and humiliation if he fails to procure a victim. Armed with this knowledge, a profiler is better able to guide police as to where someone like this would attempt to assault future victims. This is why it is so important to understand where these killers come from; it allows better prediction of future behavior.

**Multiple Murder Commonalities**

There was little academic research on serial and mass homicide in the literature before the 1800's. Prior to that point, as late as the 16th century, gruesome homicides were presumed to be the product of werewolves or other supernatural beings (Cameron & Frazer, 1987). It was believed that only a beast could inflict such brutal injuries on humans.

However, as time went by, the notion that supernatural beings committed deviant homicides evolved into the idea that "rippers" existed among the general population, terrorizing and killing innocent victims (Cameron & Frazer, 1987: 22). This progression from beast to human allowed for the categorization and study of these homicides. In other words, scholars could study the phenomenon of brutal homicide if humans were committing these terrible acts of violence. Before the crimes were attributed to human beings, they were hidden and ignored.

Time and education created a heightened awareness, which in turn led to more in-depth research. Kraft-Ebing (1901) suggested that women (who are the primary victims of brutal homicides) tended to invite their victimization. Simply, because women had low sex drives compared to men, they incited sadism in males. It was considered the victim's fault for "inciting" the lust of men with their seductive charms (Kraft-Ebing, 1901: 101). What this meant was that rage and brutality were equated with lust.

It is not surprising that these emotions are compared because they both produce very similar physiological results, one of which is arousal (Kraft-Ebing, 1901). In committing violent acts a person becomes aroused. When sexually excited, obviously arousal occurs. Such an explanation is plainly ludicrous at best and does nothing to provide comprehension of why multicide can happen. No profiles were created on the basis of this nonsense, and it was not until the early 1970's that Brittain (1970) undertook an in-depth examination of the sadistic murderer to create one of the first workable profiles.

Brittain's research focused on sexually sadistic killers because he had served as a consulting forensic psychiatrist at sadistic crime scenes for twenty years. In the study, Brittain laid out a foundation for profiling the male sexual sadist. From Brittain's experience, the sexual sadist was described as an introvert who engaged in solitary activities. He was obsessive-compulsive, shy, and felt little power in his life. He was most likely to kill when he faced stress, much like Megargee's (1966) over-controlled personality.

The male sexual sadist can appear to be a prude to the outside world, but in his internal fantasy world, he is anything but coy. The male sexual sadist enjoys a dark and violent fantasy life where he pictures various ways of torturing a victim. From tying them up to cutting them apart, many times over, with every time that he fantasizes, the image becomes more gruesome. In this fantasy world, he can be the all-powerful being that he never could be in the real world. Thus, he day-dreams as distraction. The problem begins when the fantasies no longer make the sadist feel powerful. When the sense of power is lost, in the fantasy, the sadistic killer begins searching outside of his mental realm for a victim to make him feel powerful (Langevin, 1991). Repeatedly, the fantasy cycles through the sadist's mind until he feels little choice but to act out his fantasy. In other words, the sadist's fantasy becomes his life. That's when the danger level skyrockets.

According to Brittain (1970), the sexual sadist is drawn to por-nography and other paraphernalia of cruelty, such as Nazi gear and clothing. Again, this person is seeking some form of power. He is emo-tionally flat, and, as Brittain suggests, the coldness derives from years of sickening fantasy where he dominates, tortures, and finally kills. What comes as perhaps a surprise is the high intelligence demonstrated by the sadistic killers, but one must remember, in order to create a rich, specific fantasy, one must have the faculties to do it.

Brittain also found the sadist killer to be fascinated with weapons to the point of having pet names for them. Again, the intense yearning for power is seen. Because sadistic killers connect sex with violence, it is not surprising that sadists suffer from paraphilias. A paraphilia is lit-erally an attraction to deviance. It involves intense sexual fantasies and arousal involving objects or situations that are not part of the norma-tive sexual arousal process. According to Brittain, sadistic killers had an intense interest in cross-dressing. Although many sadists would not admit to this behavior, they would admit to stealing female clothing. In the end, the preferred means of killing for the sexual sadist is strangula-tion, as it confers ultimate power to the killer: he can apply as much pressure as he desires and ultimately, determine the moment the victim will die.

Brittain's work was groundbreaking for the world of profiling (which really did not become mainstream until much later). However, it was an important piece of work that provided a strong framework for other researchers. In fact, research has consistently shown that serial murderers torture their victims for sexual gratification and power (Egger, 1985; Hickey, 1991; Holmes & DeBurger, 1988; Holmes & Holmes, 1994; Levin & Fox, 1985 67; Norris, 1988; Ressler, 1985; Rule, 1980; Sears, 1991). Often, though not always, there is a sexual component to serial murder. Thus the profile created by Brittain has been most helpful when police are faced with a sadistic killer.

### The Federal Bureau of Investigation

The Federal Bureau of Investigation (F.B.I.) began looking at multiple murderers in the late 1970's in order to create a better understanding of the people who were becoming known as serial killers. Thirty-six incarcerated sexual and serial killers were interviewed for the study. Twenty-nine were serial killers, and seven were one-time sexual killers. The study sought to examine commonalities in the lives and backgrounds of males convicted of multiple murder. These killers had exhausted all of their legal appeals, and many openly discussed their crimes, which made categorizing their crimes scenes not only possible but probable (Ressler et al., 1988).

These killers were asked questions that no one had systematically asked before, such as "How did you lure this person out of a crowded area without being noticed," or, "How did you dispose of the body," and "Why did you dispose of the body that way?" From this research, and obviously from Brittain (1970) and the work of Megargee (1966), came an F.B.I. classification of disorganized and organized offenders (see chapter 3). These categories describe certain types of homicides and the most likely type of person who would commit such a crime.

Disorganized offenders are just that: disorganized. They are unkempt individuals who kill within their residential area with weapons of opportunity (Ressler et. al., 1988). Often, the more disorganized a crime scene, the more likely the individual suffers from a psychosis (Cronin, 1996). It follows that disorganized killers are more often one-time killers than serial offenders because they are more easily caught. In contrast, the organized killer stalks, brings weapons with him, commits violence *antemortem*, and often kills outside of his residential area (Ressler et al., 1988).

Furthermore, the F.B.I. found that serial killers may be either geographically transient or stable (Holmes & DeBurger, 1985). That is, these killers either kill several people in one area (geographically stable), such as Jeffrey Dahmer who in 1992 killed several young men in his apartment in Milwaukee, or serial killers travel from place to place (geographically transient), like Ted Bundy, who in the 1970's killed over 30 women in several states. It is suggested that as society has become more mobile, a veil of anonymity serves to protect strangers and allows them to move in and out of areas without recognition (Sampson, 1987). This anonymity acts as a secret weapon for the serial killer who knows that he will fit into an area with virtually no one even giving him a second glance (Cronin, 1996). This killer is, in essence, invisible.

The F.B.I. found strong support for Brittain's (1970) earlier work on sexually-sadistic murderers. In fact, one of the most important factors in the lives of serial murderers was the intense fantasy world that these killers enjoy. Fantasy is "an elaborate thought with great preoccupation, anchored in emotion and having origins in daydreams" (Ressler et al., 1988: 72). As fantasies pertain to serial predators, researchers are most concerned with those that are "interoceptive, intrusive and reiterative" (Burgess et al., 1991: 242). That is, researchers must focus on those fantasies that are developed within the individual, persist and finally reoccur within this person's life to the point of distraction. Furthermore, these fantasies are incredibly vivid to the offender. Research has shown that the more vivid the fantasy, the more heightened the sexual response (Smither & Over, 1987). Thus it logically follows that the sexual serial murderer will fantasize with graphic details to heighten stimulation.

Research has confirmed the presence of an intense fantasy life in the world of male mass murders as well. Identifiable patterns lead to an episode of homicidal violence, and one of these patterns is a rich fantasy in which the male mass murderer seeks retribution (Kelleher, 1997). That is, the male mass murderer repeatedly thinks about killing specific individuals in order to get even for perceived wrongs. In the male mass murderer's mind, the act of multiple murder is turned into an ideal "payback" (Palermo, 1997: 3). In order to orchestrate such an extreme act of violence, the mass killer rehearses a preconceived plan that the offender has written in the mind. The killer reviews the plan repeatedly just as the male serial killer reviews his demented fantasies (Kelleher, 1997).

The fantasies appear at different times in the lives of male serial and mass murderers. For the serial killer, the fantasy life develops in early childhood and can consume a killer's life (Burgess et al., 1986; Prentky et al., 1989; Ressler et al., 1988; Reinhardt, 1957; Satten et al., 1960; Schlesinger & Revictch, 1980). An intense, rich fantasy life drives serial killers. In it, they are powerful beings who dominate everyone, and this quells reality which is far too harsh for these narcissistic beings to accept. The fantasy serves as an escape from the powerlessness, which, either in his mind or in reality, plagues the killer (Ressler et al., 1988).

Furthermore, it is through this fantasy world that the serial killer incorporates and accepts his views about sexuality. At puberty, the serial killer becomes "entrenched" in a fantasy life in which sex is twisted until, within the fantasy, there is no possibility that he could ever be rejected (Sears, 1991). The one way to ensure no rejection in the fantasy is to kill (Sears, 1991). These deviant fantasies become "fixed, negative, and repetitive" (Ressler et. al., 1988: 73). In other words, serial killers fantasize repeatedly about hurting others in order to reduce their high-tension levels. When they do so, they feel more isolated with the knowledge that what they are feeling and thinking is so different and unacceptable to society.

For the male mass murderer, the fantasies appear to come later in life, not in early childhood. The mass murderer often is seeking some type of justice when killing (Kellher, 1997). That is, killing is often motivated by revenge. The mass murderer typically perceives an injustice, which is believed to cause his downfall, but instead of immediately acting out, the mass murderer internalizes the humiliation. The injustice can be the act of being turned down for a promotion or being fired (Kelleher, 1997). The point is that the male mass murderer internalizes stress for longer periods of time than the serial killer, and this lengthy internalization leads to deviant fantasies which in turn lead to violence (Palermo, 1997). It is only after years of failure that this offender begins taking matters into the mental realm. Accordingly, serial killers and mass murderers commit multicide in order to satisfy emotional needs, and so, the motivation to kill is intrinsic (Holmes & Holmes, 1994).

### Female Killers

Interestingly, few researchers acknowledge the existence of female serial killers, and thus, not enough research has been conducted about these offenders (Cluff et al., 1997). Even though few researchers have examined the female multiple killer, it is interesting to note that Lombroso (1911) found women in general to be the worst type of sexual offender. Women seemed to be more criminal, stranger, and more sinful than men. Lombroso examined female criminals and essentially labeled them as lunatics. According to Lombroso, "female lunatics . . . surpass their male prototypes in all sexual aberrations and tendencies," (1911: 296). Humorous as this notion is, at least Lombroso took the time to analyze females, which is more than can be said for many modern-day scientists.

The same desire for power (that males aspire to) is sought with every act of homicide committed by the female, according to some theories. This is apparent through victim choice and murder method (Keppel, 1997). For example, female multiple murderers often kill with poison, and by using this method they prolong the suffering and agony of a tortured victim (Lindsay, 1958). Being slowly poisoned to death has been described as being consistently stabbed from inside the body over weeks or months (DiMaio, 1998). Nannie Doss, otherwise known as the Giggling Grandma, killed four husbands by feeding them rat poison and arsenic from 1925-1954. The victims were said to have suffered "agonizing deaths," and Nannie was said to take delight in watching the men die (Hickey, 1991: 114). One might argue that this is a very sadistic way of killing a victim, watching the victim suffering and taking delight in one's own power. In fact, Fox and Levin (1994) state that all psychopathic serial killers, male and female, are sadists who take innocent lives strictly for their own purposes.

Children as well as adults are taught that the male serial killer is not necessarily an ugly monster whom one can identify just by looking at him. In the 1970's, Ted Bundy clearly made this point because he had been described as handsome (Cronin, 1996). However, no such lessons are taught about the female offender. She is not necessarily a young, ugly, unkempt woman whom one can readily identify as criminal. She may look like a grandmother, but the serial killer is a chameleon who knows just how to behave in order to gain a person's trust (Geberth, 1998). If one is not careful, one can be lured into the serial killer's path as easily as a little child is led away from a playground.

145

### Women Who Kill

Many researchers are frustrated with the lack of knowledge when it comes to females who murder. For instance, Jones (1980: 4) states that "criminology knows next to nothing about women who kill." Furthermore, information is scant on females who commit multicide. In fact "no traditional, academic, empirical research has been attempted" concerning female serial killers (Keeney & Heide, 1994: 383). But before delving into the mind of the multiple murderer, it is helpful to understand what motivates the one-time killer.

Though there has been considerably less study on females, the research that has been done on solo female killers has demonstrated a strong connection between gender roles in society and how women carry out a murder. For instance, it has been suggested that women have been more likely to kill a powerless victim — to murder a victim while the victim was not able to defend him or herself (Wolfgang, 1958; Ward et al., 1969). This proposed what is known as "soft killings" such as those using poison, smothering or suffocation rather than hands-on, brute-force type homicides. Societal expectations suggest that women are less violent than men, and typically, they are less experienced with weapons (Wolfgang, 1958).

Females who kill one time kill close to home; that is, women kill family members. Furthermore, women tend to kill within the home itself (Blum & Fisher, 1978; Formby, 1986; Goetting, 1988; 1989; Jurik & Winn, 1990; Mann, 1996; Silverman & Kennedy, 1987; Totman, 1978). In fact, studies have shown that 80% of those who fall victim to a female killer are intimately known to her (Brown & Williams, 1993). The portrait then is a woman who strikes in close range. She is less likely than a male to roam the streets and kill a stranger; her victims will be close emotionally and physically.

Overall, the most common type of female killer is one who kills in response to a domestic violence situation. And when such a woman does lash out, she does so with a gun and hits her victim one time, no more (Formby, 1986; Goetting, 1987; Mann, 1996; McClain, 1982; Wilbanks, 1983a; 1983b). The goal in these types of homicides appears to be to put an end to the abuse without torturing the victim. This demonstrates that the typical female killer is not a predatory type. Instead, her motivation is to stop being a victim.

This is where the difference between male and female killers ends. From here, a similarity emerges. When a woman in this position (abuse victim and economically deficient) considers committing homicide, she does the same things that male multiple murderers do. She objectifies her victim, viewing the person as an object or a thing instead of a human being (Pearson, 1946). Her word choice when discussing her victims reflects this thought pattern in that she will refer to her husband as "him" or the child as "it" (Pearson, 1946). The woman then rationalizes the murder that is going to occur by telling herself: it is the only way to end her suffering. She then fantasizes about the killing, how it will be done, and what will take place upon the death (Pearson, 1946; Totman, 1978). Though she lives with violence in her mind, prior to the homicide the female is not likely to strike back physically during an abusive episode; she internalizes instead. This factor is very important as it combines with gender role expectation. Women are not supposed to be confrontational and violent. They are expected to be maternal and feminine.

**Gender Role: A Link to Murder**

Gender role places a unique and demanding stress on females because there are inherent disadvantages to being what is traditionally defined as female. Several stresses associated with gender role expectation are listed below.

- Beauty
- Sex
- Child Rearing
- Discrimination

Females still suffer from notions that beauty is all-important, and women are inundated with unrealistic stereotypes of beauty known as the "beauty myth." Strictly, most women are told that they are supposed to be beautiful, and most feel that they do not measure up to society's standards (Wolf, 1991). This creates feelings of anxiety and depression, which result in excessive spending of time and money on cosmetics, cosmetic surgery, and dieting. Such anxiety can affect self-esteem in a negative manner.

Another stress impacting women is the double standard concerning sexuality. From the time they are little, women are given one strict message about sex: they are told that "good girls don't." Sex is something that only men should do. On the other hand, as they grow and mature, women are also told that there is something wrong with those who do not engage in sexual behavior (Ogle et al., 1995). This becomes a no-win situation for females, which leads to a state of frustration and lack of control. If a single woman engages in sexual relations, she is referred to as a "slut" or "loose." If a single woman abstains from sexual behavior, she a referred to as a "prude" or "frigid." These mixed messages can have detrimental impacts of mental health.

Accordingly, the stereotype leads to a state of anxiety which many women feel can only be alleviated through marriage. When women marry, this somehow bestows "legitimacy" for sexual behavior (Ogle et al., 1995). A married woman is allowed to have sex with her husband. However, marrying does not always mitigate the emotional turmoil created by the mixed messages concerning sexuality. When women try to "legitimize" their sexual behavior by marrying, they may lose self-autonomy (control), which decreases feelings of self-worth (Bernardez-Bonesatti, 1978). In other words, by attempting to "legitimize" themselves in the public's eye, they often feel a loss of self-respect, which in turn results in depression and guilt (Bernardez-Bonesatti, 1978; Ogle et al., 1995). Simply, it is difficult to feel good about one's self when a one succumbs to peer pressure.

A third major stress linked with gender role involves motherhood. Women are often given a saint-like standard to live up to when it comes to raising children. It is assumed that women "naturally" know how to handle children, and if they do not, they are seen as unusual (Cutrona, 1984). To intensify the stress, women who work as their children grow up are vilified as uncaring, while those who stay home are left behind in the workplace. It is a double-edged sword that ensures high levels of strain and emotional turmoil for the mother. Despite these drawbacks to motherhood, a woman who does not want children is often deemed "weird," or even selfish (Wolf, 1991).

Finally, another stress for women is the discrepancy in salary between the sexes. Sadly, women often receive less salary and status in the workplace than their male counterparts. This fact alone creates risk factors that have been associated with homicide (Wolfgang, 1958). Reflect on the link between poverty and murder.

For this reason, it is important to note that females who kill one time often suffer from lack of legal and extralegal resources due to having little money (Browne & Williams, 1989). It is also known that females typically kill in an abusive situation, and they kill because they lack the resources, both monetary and social, to leave (Black, 1983). Lack of money affects resource availability, and as the female who kills one time is often unemployed or trapped in a menial job, with little education, she often has little money with which to retain legal counsel (Holmes & Holmes, 1991). When a female lacks resources, she can feel trapped and helpless to remove herself from the situation (Browne & Williams, 1989). When trapped, desperation can impact decision-making, and it is here that females are most prone to kill (Browne & Williams, 1989).

Considering the multiple stressors, one might assume that females would be more explosive and violent than men. Some researchers have suggested that the reason females are less violent is that women generally fall into a more controlled personality typology. Specifically, women are taught to turn their anger inward instead of striking out (Bernardez-Bonesatti, 1978), and this is analogous to what Megargee (1966) described as the over-controlled personality. This over-controlled personality is one who does not act out for a long time, but then, in one violent episode, this person will seemingly erupt with profound levels of violence (Megargee, 1966). This fits closely with what is known about women who kill. Most women kill in abusive situations whereby they are subjected to violence at the hands of a spouse. These women endure beatings for years until finally, they strike out and kill the abuser (Browne, 1987). So, though women experience these high levels of stress, they generally internalize the anger and hurt until they finally act out violently.

Drugs and alcohol have played a part in this violent behavior as well. It has been documented that 1/3 of females who kill use alcohol prior to the homicide (Goetting, 1989; Mann, 1996). Although previous studies indicated little drug use among female killers, only 2-3%, more recent studies show drug use at a much higher rate of 12.6% (Mann, 1996). Therefore, when women do kill, they are becoming more likely to ingest a controlled substance prior to the act.

It has also been documented that women who kill hold extremely traditional views about sex roles. That is, female killers believe that women are the caretakers who should marry, have children, and take care of the family (Bunch et al., 1983). These beliefs are strictly held, and therefore, these women "act out" these roles in their lives. They marry, they have children, and often, they do not work if they can avoid it. The goal is to be the ultimate housewife and to provide the best care for their husbands and children; fitting the stereotype of a good house-wife. This coincides with theories that relate to homicide and gender role expectation.

In summary, the general profile of women who kill is:

- Woman less than 30 years old (or in early 30's)
- Married or divorced
- Unemployed
- A mother
- High school drop out
- Economically unstable
- Unable to cope with stress

The female killer is often found in a destructive relationship, with few skills, and is isolated with little emotional support. She considers murder because she feels a lack of alternatives (Pearson, 1946). After all, she has few marketable skills with which to support herself. She has locked herself into a very traditional sex role being a housewife — not working outside the home or obtaining higher education. When a woman kills, she often does so because she feels hopeless and unhappy (Ogle et al., 1995). Stresses have built up over the years, and as she has placed herself in a very conservative "female" role, she has no outlet for her anger. She has turned this anger inward into depression and low self-esteem (Bernardez-Bonesatti, 1978). In our society, a woman's suc-cess is often measured in terms of juggling a successful marriage and family.

It is significant that a woman would choose to kill those inti-mately known to her. Her family defines who she is, so when she kills them, she is thus killing her own identity (Totman, 1978). When she kills, a woman does not like who she has become. Through the killing, she wishes to restore happiness (or at least the illusion of happiness) that apparently can only come if she is rid of the individual or individuals who are troubling her (Hartman, 1977).

This is logical, in a way, since women often kill in an "explosion," and their victims are typically family members. Researchers have also found that women who kill are older than their male counterparts. Males who kill are usually young, ranging from late teens to early 20's. Female killers, on the other hand, have an age range of late 20's to early 30's (Totman, 1978). This lends more credibility to the view that women let anger simmer for long periods of time before they kill. The aforementioned characteristics comprise the solo killer, but such research has not been conducted effectively with females who kill more than one person.

### Child-Killers

Women are far more likely than men to be the killers of children. From the beginnings of time, women have been saddled with child-rearing responsibilities, which sometimes can be more than overwhelming. In a bad moment, a horrid act can take place, and a death can occur. At one point in our history, there appeared to be a plethora of child killings. In fact, in the 18th century, infanticide was so common that criminal penalties had to be reduced due to the sheer number of offenders committing the crime (Empey, 1978; Jones, 1980).

What made this phenomenon so common? Devaluation of illegitimate children was a primary element. In the early 19th century, illegitimate children essentially had no place in society and were considered worthless. Birth control methods being far from what they are today, the possibility of becoming pregnant was great. When an unmarried woman became pregnant, the message sent by society was that she could not keep a bastard, yet she could not give the child away either (Empey, 1978). Just what the woman was supposed to do was never mentioned, so it was a no win situation for an unwed mother. Many women, not wanting to bear the expense or notoriety of a "worthless" child, chose homicide as a route of escape (Rose, 1986). There was a feeling of helplessness, a lack of alternatives, which should sound familiar as a motivating force for homicide in general.

## The Categories

Over the years, females who kill children have been separated into one of two categories:

- Insane
- Evil

Typically, those who fall into the insane category kill a child who is under the age of 12 months. When women kill such a young child, the act is assumed to be one erupting from a psychosis (Wilczynski, 1991). How else could a woman come to kill a defenseless baby? She must be insane. In such cases, courts tend to be more lenient than in other situations because the females are viewed with compassion for the plight that centers on a break with reality (Wilczynski, 1991). Insanity is excusable, for the insane don't know what they're doing.

In the last decade, researchers have paid particular attention to one form of mental disorder that drives infanticide. This is called "Munchausen Syndrome By Proxy". The disorder is characterized by a persistent desire to attract attention by harming a child, and it is most often exhibited by parents (Boros & Brubaker, 1992). The individual who suffers from the disorder receives a sense of importance and self-worth from harming a child, then "saving" the infant by rushing the child to medical care (Artingstall, 1995).

Specifically, those who suffer from Munchausen Syndrome By Proxy will make repeated trips to the emergency room with the injured child, while remaining calm during the process. The calm demeanor is unusual for a parent in such a situation. At the same time, the person with this disorder will be ever-vigilant and remain by the child's bed-side. Then strangely, when the child begins to recover, the individual becomes agitated (Boros & Brubaker, 1992).

If the mother who kills her child is not judged insane, she is placed into the second (and more ridiculed) category of child-murderer. This is the "bad" or "evil" category. Such child-killers are viewed with contempt because they are perceived as callous, cold, and selfish (Wilczynski, 1991). Instead of breaking with reality or snapping due to insanity, the women in this category plan their murders. Some researchers have even referred to such women as monsters (Edwards, 1986). Such an attitude is developed by the perception that "good" mothers protect and care for their children. Accordingly, some re-searchers have concluded that if one is not "good," one must be "bad" (Wilczynski, 1991). If a female is placed into this category, she will be treated harshly by the criminal justice system; but if she is placed into the insane category, she is more likely to be treated with compassion. Though the result is the same (murder), the intent is con-sidered in sentencing.

In summary, a composite has been created of the type of woman most likely to kill her baby. She is a woman who married young, lived in isolation with the child, and in many instances had no desire for the child in the first place (Straus, 1986). She was also likely to be a woman with little money who abused her child before she killed the child (Mann, 1996). When this woman finally decided to kill, she killed with her hands. She strangled or smothered her baby because such murder methods are difficult to detect (Mann, 1996; Weisheit, 1986). It appears that poverty, inexperience, loneliness, and anger drive this phenomenon of killing a child. The female child killer is a woman who felt trapped with an unwanted financial burden. Because of inadequate financial resources and inadequate emotional coping skills, the female child killer committed murder to escape her situation.

## Multiple Murder Typologies

Since it is clear, upon analyzing the one-time killer, that there are common factors associated with the crime, similar typologies have been developed for the female multiple murderer.

1. HOLMES: Holmes and Holmes (1994) describe five different types of female multiple murderers:

- Visionary
- Comfort
- Hedonistic
- Power/control
- Disciple.

**Visionary.** The first and easiest type to explain is the visionary killer. This killer murders in response to voices or visions that command that she kill (Holmes & Holmes, 1994). A perfect example of a psychotic, the visionary killer cannot discern the difference between hallucinations and reality. Priscilla Ford is an excellent example of a female visionary mass murderer. In 1982, Ford drove her Lincoln Continental down a Reno, Nevada sidewalk, killing several people. A former teacher, she had suffered an obvious break with reality; she stated that God commanded her to kill. She believed that the people she ran over were bad and needed to die.

**Comfort.** The second type of female multiple murderer is the comfort killer. This type of murderer is better known than the visionary killer because the motivation is common. The comfort killer murders for financial reasons, and several female serial killers fit within this category. This is the woman who kills those around her and collects her victim's benefits and insurance money. For instance, in 1976, Janice Gibbs killed her husband, three sons, and her grandson for thousands of dollars of insurance money (Holmes & Holmes, 1994). She was sentenced to five consecutive life sentences in Georgia. Similarly, in 1988, Dorothea Puente reportedly murdered nine elderly people, buried them in her Sacramento, California, back yard, then collected their social security checks (Wood, 1994). By killing their victims and collecting money, these women fit into a comfort-killer typology.

**Hedonistic.** The third female multiple killer is the hedonistic killer. A hedonist is one who seeks pleasure, and the hedonistic killer murders for sexual pleasure. Because there are so few, this is the least understood of the female killers (Holmes & Holmes, 1994). The hedonistic murderer kills for pleasure and sexual gratification. One may argue that Karla Faye Tucker (who killed two people with a pickaxe) was such a killer. Karla Faye allegedly admitted to having several orgasms as she hacked at her victims with the deadly instrument (A&E Special Reports, 1998). Certainly Tucker made the connection between violence and sex making her a hedonistic killer.

**Power/Control.** The fourth type is the power-seeker. This person is one who wants control over life and death. She wants recognition, and she seeks it in a most unusual way. This is akin to the Munchausen Syndrome By Proxy killer. She will intentionally cause a helpless victim to stop breathing either by putting a pillow over the face or injecting some drug into the victim's system. Then, she will call attention to the dying victim whom she works hard to "rescue" so she can look like a hero. This type of killer is more often a nurse or caregiver. An example would be a mother who repeatedly brings her asphyxiated baby to the emergency room so she can get attention from the hospital staff.

**Disciple.** Finally, the last type of multiple killer is the disciple killer. The disciple acts under the influence of a charismatic leader (Holmes and Holmes, 1994). She kills because she is so influenced by a powerful individual that she will do whatever that person bids her to do. Leslie Van Houten and Susan Atkins participated in a murder that had been ordered by their cult "leader" Charles Manson in 1969. The process is like brainwashing, in which the female is separated from family and friends so she becomes increasingly dependent on the leader. Ever so slowly, she comes to believe that the leader is all-powerful and must be followed at all costs.

**2. KELLEHER:** Kelleher (1998) sought to classify female serial killers into specific typologies. Four of the Holmes types were used as well as three additional categories

- Hedonistic (though he titles this group: the sexual predators),
- Comfort (entitled for profit and black widows),
- Visionary (called question of sanity)
- Power seeker (angel of death).

Kelleher then adds the categories:

- Revenge
- Team
- Unexplained

**Revenge.** The revenge killer is one who kills to achieve retribution from someone or for something. This killer targets family members, and the motivation is very personal (Kelleher, 1998). It is an emotional drive (anger) that compels the revenge killer to plan and execute murder in a serial fashion. Though she plans over an extended period of time, she lacks the flat emotion that enables the more typical serial killer to kill over long periods of time. Simply, her emotions get in her way because they cloud her judgment, and she does not plan as extensively as a "black widow". She acts more spontaneously than other killers, thus making mistakes. In the early 1990's, Martha Ann Johnson was convicted in the deaths of her four children after she allegedly suffocated each child, following an argument with her husband. In a confession, she stated that she killed the children in order to punish her husband, or for revenge (Kelleher, 1998).

**Team.** The team killer was Kelleher's next category, and this is an extremely important segment. To put this in perspective, most team killers consist of female/male teams. That is, when a female and male engage in multiple murder together, they are part of the largest percentage of team killers (Kelleher, 1998). The female in this type of team is, typically, younger than her male counterpart, and she is submissive to him. She us typically tied to this man by a sexual relationship, and this sexual relationship carries over to the killing. The team most often abducts females, who are then raped and killed by the team (Kelleher, 1998). Both participate. Both kill.

**Unexplained.** This segment includes the female "who systematically murders for reasons that are wholly inexplicable or for a motive that has not been made sufficiently clear for categorization,"(Kelleher, 1998: 173).

## Current Research

The boundary between hypotheses and concrete data is thick. Thus, these existing typologies, though useful in speculation, do not provide homicide detectives and researchers with nearly enough information to elucidate motivations. The following provides actual data from research interviews conducted by the author. Following is a point-by-point crime scene comparison between female and male multiple killers.

## Common Characteristics

Specific characteristic patterns are seen in the lives of adult females who commit multiple murder. From marital status to appearance, a solid picture of these killers has emerged.

By the time the female multiple murderer reaches adulthood, she typically is a divorced woman. In fact, of the seven women interviewed for this research, all but one were divorced in their twenties. However, most of these women did not remarry. It seemed that after suffering from a failed marriage, the female multiple murderer became increasingly isolated, afraid of being hurt. Most often, there is no immediate family or friends from whom she can garner support. The females in this study reported high levels of anxiety and depression at the prospect of being alone, and as previously noted, one of the hallmarks of the multicidal offender is the inability to cope with stress. Being left alone with few marketable skills, the female is put into a powerless position.

Working, however, seemed to put too much strain on these females. Only four of the women involved in this research held legal jobs in their lifetimes, and of those, not one remained at a job for over two years. That is, it was unusual for the females in this sample to remain employed at one location for any substantial length of time. The remaining three women either did not work at all or were engaged in illicit and unsteady employment such as prostitution.

Since they had no higher education, the female multiple murderers in this sample were unemployable as far as high-paying jobs. These women had no qualms about being unemployed and using other means to obtain money; they sought money through illegal means such as theft or prostitution.

It was important that the women appear well groomed and feminine. This is very interesting as female multiple murderers kill while in gender-specific roles (care giving). Being a woman, looking feminine, was extremely important. Reasons given were "I wanted to look like a lady," and "that's what girls do." One can see clearly defined gender roles.

For this reason, by the time the female multiple murderer reached adulthood, she had better control over her weight. Of the seven women involved in this research, only one remained overweight in adulthood, and she was only slightly overweight. It appears that the desire to look feminine and attractive outbalanced the temptation to overeat. When asked how they managed their weight, all seven reported eating special diets. None reported a regular exercise routine, which is consistent with their behaviors in childhood. Each woman was asked why she did not exercise regularly, and the replies centered around the urge to avoid social interaction. Their perception of exercise included going to a gym, and they did not wish to spend time in a gym with other people.

One of the main reasons that the females put such a premium on looking attractive was the desire to become attached to a lover. However, as they aged, they found the supply of eligible men dwindling. Whereas the women could turn to older men when they were teenagers, after being divorced and left without job prospects, they found themselves with fewer options. After all, the woman typically has little education and little tolerance for working at a job that requires an eight-hour day. She has no car. She has few social skills and prefers solitude. She has a sour outlook in life. Not the most attractive catch, for a man.

Upon being rejected, feelings of powerlessness and hopelessness set in, and increased isolation occurs once again. When they were children, and when isolation levels increased, there was a tendency to turn inward into a violent fantasy world. In the fantasy, the female is all-powerful which serves as an escape. Once the fantasies could no longer create feelings of serenity, the female multiple murderers expressed these fantasies in the forms of predatory and violent behavior: killing cats; harming other children. However, these acts become tiresome and unfulfilling. Progression is inevitable. Once the females are rejected and left with little prospect of obtaining money or a partner, the wheels of murder are set into motion. This is when the danger line is crossed. It is here that the female turns to multiple murder.

**Homicide Analysis**

The homicides committed by females can be classified using the F. B.I.'s dichotomy of organized and disorganized characteristics. Organized offenders planned their offenses, brought weapons with them, restrained victims, and took efforts to conceal the victims' bodies. Disorganized offenders tended not to plan their crimes, left evidence at crime scenes, and did not conceal bodies (Ressler et al., 1988).

As it applies to females:

Mass murderers ------------------Disorganized
Serial killers-------------------------Organized.

These female mass murderers:

- Range in age from 19-35
- Are less attentive to appearance than serial killers
- Appear to have average intelligence
- Dropped out of high school
- Left messy crime scenes

These female serial killers:

- Exhibit social competence
- Worked at care-giving jobs
- Planned the offenses
- Controlled their mood during the crimes
- Experienced a precipitating stress prior to the crimes
- Showed interest in the news media after the crimes
- Essentially hid the bodies

Female mass murderers resemble the disorganized offender in almost every way. Their crimes tend to be spontaneous, without planning, and they acquire the weapon at the scene. Victims are simply in the wrong place at the wrong time, and there is a great deal of trauma to the body. The female takes no steps to hide her identity and leaves physical evidence behind.

One may ask why she would do this. The answer is that she didn't plan on committing the crime. It is a situation where the female has allowed stress build to the point of explosion. There is a trigger, a stressful event, which serves to strike the match and begin the killing. The female perpetrator's mindset is that she has nothing to lose. She is unemployed, poor, without friends and family, and she finds herself alone. She has no skills to market, and in her eyes, there is no job that she can find. Her own life is useless; therefore, anyone's life is useless. She objectifies her victims, projects her own feelings of worthlessness onto the victims, and begins killing.

Once she has finished committing her murders, she simply walks away without attempting to wipe away evidence or hide herself. She feels that her life is over anyway, so if she gets caught, it doesn't really matter. At this point, she tends to be agitated, yet calm. The killings have served a purpose to her, to alleviate her stress. It is at this point that she goes home and goes to sleep.

The serial killer is a very different creature and arguably much more dangerous. This is the offender who thinks about killing for long periods of time and meticulously plans each offense. Remarkably, the serial killer is callous and unaffected by the suffering of her victims. She educates herself about autopsy methods so that she can attempt to kill without anyone knowing that a homicide has taken place. She poisons or asphyxiates her victims (who are known to her). She presents herself as a friend to her victims, while considering each person's weaknesses

| Table 7-1 Profile Characteristics Of Organized Offenders | |
|---|---|
| **Male Organized Killer** | **Female Serial Killer** |
| Good Intelligence | Good Intelligence |
| Socially Competent | Socially Competent |
| Skilled Work Preferred | Skilled Work Preferred |
| Sexually Competent | Sexually Competent |
| High Birth Order Status | N/A |
| Father's Work Stable | N/A |
| Inconsistent Childhood Discipline | Inconsistent Childhood Discipline |
| Controlled Mood During Crime | Controlled Mood During Crime |
| Use of Alcohol With Crime | N/A |
| Precipitating Situation Stress | Precipitating Situation Stress |
| Living With Partner | N/A |
| Mobility Follows News Media | N/A Follows News Media |
| May Change Jobs or Leave Town | N/A |
| Offense Planned | Offense Planned |
| Victim a Stranger* | Victim Known* |
| Personalizes Victim | Personalizes Victim |
| Controlled Conversation | Controlled Conversation |
| Crime Scene Reflects Control | Crime Scene Reflects Control |
| Demands Submissive Victim | Demands Helpless Victim |
| Restraints | No Restrains Necessary (de facto) |
| Aggressive Acts Prior to Death | N/A |
| Body Hidden | Body Essentially Hidden |
| Weapon Absent | Weapon Absent |
| Transports Victim | N/A |

N/A No Basis for Comparison
* Denotes Differences

| Table 7-2 Profile Characteristics Of Disorganized Offenders | |
| --- | --- |
| **Male Disorganized Killer** | **Female Mass Killer** |
| Fairly Intelligent | Average Intelligence |
| Socially Immature | Socially Immature |
| Poor Work History | Poor Work History |
| Sexually Incompetent | N/A |
| Youngest Child | Youngest Child |
| Inconsistent Discipline | Inconsistent Discipline |
| Abusive Parents | Abusive Parents |
| Anxious Mood During Crime | Anxious Mood During Crime |
| Minimal Use of Alcohol* | Heavy Use of Alcohol* |
| Minimal Situation Stress | Minimal Situation Stress |
| Living Alone | N/A |
| Living Near Crime | Living Near Crime |
| Minimal Interest in Media | Modest Interest in Media |
| Minimal Changes in Lifestyle* | No Changes in Lifestyle* |
| Spontaneous Offense* | Less Planned Offense* |
| Victim Known | Victim Known |
| Depersonalizes Victim | Depersonalizes Victim |
| Minimal Conversation W/Victim | Minimal Conversation W/Victim |
| Crime Scene Sloppy | Crime Scene Sloppy |
| Sudden Violence | Sudden Violence |
| Minimal Use of Restraints* | No Use of Restraints* |
| Sexual Acts After Death | N/A |
| Body Left in Plain View | Body Left in Plain View |
| Evidence | Evidence |
| Body Left at Death Scene | Body Left at Death Scene |

N/A No Basis for Comparison
* Denotes Differences

and how those weaknesses can be exploited. Once a victim trusts her, the female serial killer ensures that the victim is vulnerable, and then she kills. She ensures that no one else is present and takes great pains to make sure that the body looks untouched. That way, there will at least be a question as to whether the death was natural or something else. The serial killer is flat (without animation) when questioned, and this should serve as an indicator for police.

However, most often law enforcement officials do not recognize the deaths as homicides because they are staged so well. The serial killers do not use restraints because their victims are helpless (the victims are essentially restrained by being in a hospital bed, or by virtue of old age or extreme youth). When the death is discovered, there are no outward signs of foul play. Therefore, many times police are not involved at all. The female who has committed the murder is emotionally cold and unresponsive to guilt. Those emotions simply do not work on the serial killer, so the female can proceed with her life without showing outward signs of stress, which might otherwise be indicative of homicidal involvement. She moves on, and the death is often ruled natural.

- No one knows there has been a homicide.
- The female begins looking for another victim.

**Male versus Female**

These classifications of organized/disorganized are directly taken from the F.B.I.'s studies on male offenders. Notice the direct similarities when comparing point by point. Table 7-1 examines the organized characteristics of male and female serial killers. Table 7-2 examines this disorganized typology as it applies to female mass murderers and male serial killers.

**Case Study: Organized Offender**

Cassandra (pseudonym) was born in the 1920's into a world that didn't want her. She was the sixth child of seven, destined to be cast out. Her father was gravely ill and spewed verbal acid at his children, claiming that all people were bad. So Cassandra's mother picked up the slack and worked in the fields picking fruits and vegetables. The children were not spared hardship, for they worked in the fields too. Every day from sunup to sundown, the children would toil with their hands.

Though they worked, it wasn't long before the kids were too much of a strain on their parents. Cassandra's mother would lock the children in dark closets, sometimes for days, while she caroused in town for fun. The children's father was a helpless sick man who had no interest in looking after his kids, so he let his wife do whatever she wanted with the little ones.

Cassandra developed difficulty speaking, stuttering at various times while growing up. This led to merciless teasing by other children; and that drove her into a private world where she was in control. Cassandra became a consummate liar, capable of spinning the most ridiculous tales at will. She'd learned that in order to get what you want, you must lie, and her lies entertained anyone who would listen. At school she was relegated to the back of the room because she was overly quiet and stayed away from other children. She had an unusual habit of hanging on other children when she could grab onto them, and for no apparent reason, she became very ill herself. Doctors could find nothing wrong with her, yet she constantly complained of various sicknesses. After a while, people started ignoring her whenever she claimed to be under the weather, and she invented a new story about being the daughter of very rich parents in order to keep attention.

Cassandra was raped, beaten, and told that she was worthless, all before age 7, when her father died. She described her childhood as "hellish," and was happy in prison as opposed to being with her parents. Her family moved constantly, so Cassandra never made close friends. In fact, whenever her family would move into a new town, Cassandra found enjoyment in stalking little animals and killing them. She did it because she saw the other children playing with the animals, and she figured, if she could take the animals away, the other children would be as miserable as her. But the killing didn't make her feel any better, so she started wondering what it might be like to kill another person. Her thoughts were filled with images of her making others die.

By age 9, Cassandra was left in an orphanage. Her mother was running wild, typically in a drunken stupor, and her father was dead. Cassandra couldn't stand the horrible living arrangement at the orphanage, so she started running away. She would become friendly with older men who briefly took care of her in turn for sexual favors. Then when her charms ran out, she'd return. Desperate to get out of her life, at age 16, she married a man several years older. She had become a prostitute, known for being "cold." But her new husband adored her and actually approved of her prostitution. Being from misery, Cassandra tried everything she could think of to black it out, but nothing seemed to work. Within one year, she had given birth to a little girl whom she seemed to detest. People remarked that she never wanted to be near her child. In fact, she sent her off to live with distant relatives just so she didn't have to see her — so it was surprising when Cassandra had another child just two years later. Like her sister before her, she was sent off and put up for adoption.

During her marriage and the birth of her two daughters, Cassandra suffered from terrible nightmares that disturbed her sleep. It seemed impossible for her to get one sound night's rest, so she turned to alcohol in order to make her sleepy. But this was not a solution, and her drinking became worse. She was having dark thoughts about killing people; her life was going nowhere. Then things got worse. Her husband left her because he couldn't stand her drinking and her lying. So, her life was beginning to be as miserable as it was while she was growing up.

Cassandra didn't fold, though. She resumed selling her body for money and was always able to con someone out of what she needed. But her first major arrest came shortly, when she stole some checks. She plea-bargained her way to a minimal sentence. Again she resumed prostituting herself when she was released, and she found herself another husband. The marriage was horrible from the start. The pair fought constantly, because Cassandra would run off for long periods of time, and her husband never knew where she went or what she was doing. But Cassandra had built up a business for herself. She was a madam who ran a whorehouse from 9:00-5:00, in an attempt to make it appear like a legitimate business. Cassandra was arrested once again in a police sting operation, and this was the last straw for her second husband, who promptly divorced her upon discovering her arrest.

Now life was not so bad for Cassandra, who was determined to make a living for herself. She was a savvy businesswoman who knew the justice system and how to manipulate others. It didn't take long for her to begin preying on the helpless. She moved to a southern city and began taking in the homeless and the sick. Her goal was to take their money and embezzle it, a plan that worked successfully almost from the start. This was a great scam for a con artist who was so good at lying and stealing that it was often too late when her marks realized that they had been taken in — in more ways than one. At the same time Cassandra found herself yet another husband, this time a good-looking young man who was out for a meal ticket. It was a mere matter of weeks before Cassandra discovered that she didn't like being a "sugar daddy" and quickly divorced her third husband.

From that point on, Cassandra was driven to acquire as much money as she could. She loved buying expensive perfumes and luxury items, but the money she scammed from her few boarders was not enough to maintain her lavish lifestyle. There had to be more money somewhere. As she contemplated her options, she realized that if she killed her boarders and kept their deaths secret, she could still receive their benefit checks — if she was designated to receive the money on behalf of the victims. In other words, if Cassandra could convince her victims to sign over their benefit checks to her, then she could kill the victims and still collect their checks. It was a wonderful plan, and Cassandra developed it in painstaking detail. She read up on murder and the least-detectable ways to kill. What she found was that she could dispose of a person with poison without getting caught. One by one, her boarders started disappearing, yet Cassandra kept cashing their checks. No one missed the poor victims, and it wasn't until an acquaintance tipped off police that Cassandra's reign of murder came to an end. In total, nine victims were discovered.

### Offender Preparation

Cassandra had thought about killing for a long time and was certain that she did not want to be apprehended for her actions. So she read about murder, the police, and how to kill without being detected. After studying her craft for years, she discovered that poisoning someone who was very sick or very old was unlikely to arouse police suspicion. At most, the death would pass as natural. Cassandra was clever and quickly realized that if she poisoned the sick and elderly who were poor and had no family, even fewer questions would be raised concerning their deaths. These facts tipped her over the edge to kill. Cassandra searched out victims and obtained as may prescriptions as she could. It was then that she slowly poisoned her victims with lethal combinations of narcotics.

### Victims

Cassandra selected her victims carefully. Each potential victim had to meet several criteria in order to be targeted for murder. First, the victim had to be poor. Second, it was essential that the victim not have family close by. Third, the victims had to be elderly and/or ill. With this criteria met, Cassandra risked very little when killing. Such victims are not easily missed and often are overlooked by the criminal justice system.

Murders

Cassandra chose the "safest" way to kill. Her method of murder was covert, meaning that there were no obvious signs of trauma to the bodies. She carefully poisoned her victims over time and disposed of their bodies by burying them so that they would not be missed. As time progressed, Cassandra's taste for blood increased, and she killed more often and began mutilating the bodies *postmortem*. When the bodies were discovered, medical examiners were unable to determine if some of the wounds inflicted were *ante* or *postmortem*.

Overview

Cassandra was an organized serial killer who planned and prepared for a great deal of time before committing her crimes. She chose a weapon, thought about how to use it, and considered the least-risk body disposal method. Cassandra made sure that her murder method was covert and that it would be difficult for law enforcement to determine that a homicide had occurred. She was methodical in her handling of the bodies and left little physical evidence behind. It was imperative that she conceal her crimes, and by burying the bodies, she made evidence retrieval even more difficult.

**Case Study: Disorganized Offender**

Brenda (pseudonym) was born into a family with one older brother. Her mother was described as ultra-feminine and incapable of sustaining herself without a man to support her. Brenda's parents were unmarried, and her father was a high-ranking member of a biker gang. The family was homeless on a regular basis because Brenda's mother didn't work, and her father only had money when he stole it. There was no positive working model for Brenda to follow.

Her home life can be characterized as extremely abusive. Brenda was sodomized at the age of two and was repeatedly raped by her father and members of the biker gang up until she ran away from home at age 12. Her father tortured her by burning her on a hot furnace and beating her. Additionally, the children in this area were forced to fight much as dogs or roosters are pitted against one another. If they refused to fight, they were beaten by the adults. This is where Brenda learned to use a knife and gun. It was common in this group for the children to carry weapons. Brenda started carrying a knife by age 9.

School was difficult for the young girl who knew nothing but violence, and she did not excel academically. She purposely sat in the back of the classroom and stayed away from other children unless she wanted to fight. She wasn't allowed to have friends, so she spent most of her time alone in a junkyard, where she began stalking small animals. Cats were her choice target, and when asked why, she responded that "they were there."

By the time Brenda entered early adolescence, she was smoking and drinking on a regular basis. She started having sex with young boys at age 11, but she had a secret desire to sleep with women. Accordingly, she admits to sexually assaulting a female schoolmate when she was 12 years old. The girl did not report the incident because Brenda threatened her life with the knife she kept in her pocket.

Brenda had gained a reputation for being a drug-using fighter, and to earn money, she sold her body to older men. She stated that she didn't mind having sex with men, but she simply preferred women. Money was the goal, and Brenda also robbed her customers at gunpoint. On two occasions, she tried to kill male customers. She stabbed each man several times, just for fun, but the men lived. They, too, did not report the incidents because they were fearful that Brenda would find and kill them. By this time, Brenda had married a man who supported her, but the marriage was doomed from the start. They separated within a few months but never got divorced.

Brenda did not graduate from high school, and she had no job skills. However, she did have a seething hatred of people, and many times she had thought about killing and how she would do it. She was considered "bad news" by people on the street because she had such a violent reputation. Once she had grown up, even tough members of the biker gang stayed away from her. Brenda's quick temper was known and respected. But things did not improve for the young woman who had nothing. Instead, they got worse. She took up with another woman and got more heavily involved in heavy drugs. She sold her body as well as drugs, and most days she spent in a drugged stupor. When she finally decided to kill, she wasn't going to do it halfway and leave a chance for her victims to live. Unlike her earlier attempts, she was going to make sure that her victims died, this time. Brenda was arrested and was sentenced to death for the murders of five men and women.

Offender Preparation

Brenda did not elaborately plan out her murders. In fact, it was more spur of the moment than anything else. Her temper got the better of her, that day. She was still a teenager when she captured her victims and committed multiple murder. She had been taking drugs nonstop for several days prior to the murders, and she did not bring a weapon with her when she engaged her victims.

Victims

Brenda was careful as to whom she selected. All of her victims were much older and were feeble. It did not matter to her whether they were male or female. In fact, she killed both. As her crime began, she got into an argument with one of the victims (whom she knew) and took his gun. At that point, she forced him into his car along with four other victims.

Murders

Brenda shot her victims in the head after driving them around town for several hours. She took them to a vacant field and ordered them to lie on the ground. It was there that she shot them, one by one. They did not die. After being shot, they were forced back into the car, driven to different locations, then forced out again and killed. Brenda was unrepentant for her crimes and simply walked away after shooting her victims. She made no attempts to hide herself from police. She also did not try to destroy evidence. Upon arrest, she was described as belligerent and cold. She even went so far as to try to force her cellmate to exchange clothes with her so she could get out of her bloodstained shirt.

Overview

Brenda did not plan her crimes. The propensity to kill had been building within her for a long time before she successfully killed her victims. She did enjoy violent fantasy and did carry a weapon. However, she was not carrying a weapon the day she committed the murders. Instead, she spontaneously took the gun from her victim and then chose her victims by chance. In other words, her victims were not stalked, and the murders were not planned. Brenda did not attempt to conceal her identity nor did she try to destroy evidence. She simply walked away from her crimes and proceeded as if nothing had happened. This is typical of a disorganized offender.

## Antemurder and Postmurder

Stress affects us all. From noisy children to angry bosses, we live in a world where our tension tolerance is tested on a regular basis. But for the female multiple murderer, stress pushes them too far. They have no skills to cope when placed under duress, and when stresses build, a dangerous situation is created.

It is well known that male multiple murderers are instigated by a pre-crime stressor. Something happens that sets them off. This is true for women, as well. Within a few months prior to the homicides, a

| Table 6-10 Homicide Characteristics | | |
|---|---|---|
| Characteristic | Number/Total | Percent |
| Pre-Crime Stress | 7/7 | 100 |
| Vulnerable Victim | 7/7 | 100 |
| Power Feeling | 6/7 | 87.0 |
| Detached Manner | 5/7 | 71.0 |
| Post-Crime Relief | 5/7 | 71.0 |
| Funeral Attendance | 4/7 | 57.0 |
| Media Fascination | 4/7 | 57.0 |
| Trophy | 4/7 | 57.0 |

stressful event occurred in the females' lives. These events included receiving past due notices on accounts, being forced to take their children (whom they had abandoned) into their homes, having intense arguments with family members, and being placed in a position where they were forced to watch someone in a happy situation.

This latter stressor deserves further examination because it is crucial. In several cases, the women were living or working with an individual who appeared to have everything that the female multiple murderer could not have. Being in close proximity and watching a person live a happy life was upsetting to the point of distraction. They knew they were different and could not have things such as love, money, and security. It appeared as if a positive event *in the life of someone else,* who is in close proximity to the female multiple killer, served as a stressor to the female killer. The positive events included a marriage and a pregnancy.

The women stated that it was unbearable to watch someone else get what they felt they should have. Therefore, in response, they chose to kill an innocent victim.

The selection process, that is, determining who would die, depended on the female killer's circumstances. If a child was in her care, and she knew that no one could observe her actions, she was likely to kill that child. The same selection process took place for those who killed victims (other than children) in their care. It was simply a matter of convenience and a determination of whether suspicion would be raised upon the death. For those killers who did not murder someone in their care, victim selection appeared to be a matter of availability. In other words, if a victim was in the path of the female multiple murderer, the victim was killed. In all instances, it appeared as if victim selection was a matter of convenience. Furthermore, the victims were observed prior to death, and in fact, all victims conversed with their killers prior to death. The question seemed to be, "Who can I kill without being caught?" Table 6-10 displays the homicide characteristics.

When first asked about their crimes, most of the women claimed faulty memories. It took several hours of building rapport before the women felt comfortable enough to discuss what actually occurred when they murdered their victims. Most commonly, the act was described as occurring in slow motion, and the women recalled the crimes in graphic detail. What was fascinating was the way that the women characterized their parts in the crimes. Apparently, the act of strangling, suffocating, stabbing, or shooting was deemed as being "robotic." In other words, female multiple murderers act in a detached, rote manner. There was no feeling of sadness for the victims as they were killed,

nor was there excessive anger. One woman described the acts of murder like this:

> I didn't think it'd be that easy, you know that I'm saying? I
> mean, who'd think you could put your hands like this
> (demonstrates her hands around her neck) and squeeze? I
> mean, I never thought it'd be easy. I mean, it didn't take
> much time for her, the one I was charged with, it didn't take
> much time. People ask me what'd you feel like when you
> were doing it, and all I can say is I didn't feel nothing. She
> was a thing to me, you know what I mean? She was dead
> before I did it. Does that sound bad? I'm not a bad person.

When asked why it was so easy, this same convicted serial killer
responded:

> I think it was the way I was, my mind was working. I think
> it happened when I was seven, and she (stepmother) locked
> me in the closet again. I didn't have nothing else to do. What
> would you do? Wouldn't you think about being someplace
> else, and you being with the key (to the closet)? I, you don't
> know what it was like for me in, I'm not a bad person. You'd
> think about killing people too if you were, if that happened
> to you. I'm not different from you. You'd think about it too.

Apparently this particular serial killer wanted to create some sort
of kinship between us. She tried very hard to convince me that she was
a good person who had simply been put in a bad circumstance. However, she did go on to describe her fantasies:

> Me and, it didn't matter who, but me, that's what was im-
> portant. I was the one in my fantasies. I was, I could do what
> I wanted to her (stepmother). It started out, like, it's like a
> fairytale, you know? It would start out with me in the closet,
> you know? Then I'd have, I'd be the one locking kids in the

closet, and I'd get to listen to them scream, um, I know how that sounds. But when I'd get mad, I'd, the closet was where it happened. I'd go into that world much of my time. (Laughs). You know, when I'd get mad, you, uh, you didn't want to be near me because I was mean, um, and I could do anything I wanted, you know? It, um, all of it started in the closet, but it'd end up as me being the one putting my hands on her (stepmother) throat. (Expletive), I did that so much of time it was easy when I put my hands on (first victim's) throat.

So it appears as though the continuous rehearsals in the fantasies made the women more proficient when committing the actual crimes. The fantasies were important and ritualistic. There appears to have been a triggering event that forced the female into her mental realm where she could be in control of the situation. The triggering event typically involved some type of altercation with someone who had power over the female. Whether it was a parent, teacher, or bigger child, the females were made to feel powerless — the impetus for retreat into violent fantasy.

All five recalled feeling at peace after the murders; the homicides served as a mechanism to relieve their high stress levels. "I went home and slept," was a common quote (5/5). "I knew everything would be all right," said one mass murderer. Of those five who discussed their crimes, all went about their daily lives in a normal way following the crimes. There was clean up, if necessary, but not one of them panicked after the crimes. Four women attended their victims' funerals — and all four were serial killers. It should be noted that those who did not attend the funerals were in jail for the crimes (mass murderers).

For those four who were not immediately apprehended after their crimes, all reported going to work the day after the homicides. There were no outward signs of distress. When asked why not, they indicated that they had thought about committing the acts in their heads for so long, that they had considered almost everything that would happen. In most instances, they were correct in estimating how events would unfold, and so they were prepared. This led to feelings of power and comfort.

Accordingly, it was common for the female serial killer to read about and collect news items regarding their crimes (4/4). One woman even went so far as to make a scrapbook, complete with her own notes about how much she enjoyed watching the confusion of police and medical personnel. This offender asked the author if copies of autopsy photos of her victims could be brought to the interview. This request was not granted. Though she did not admit to it, it is likely that she wanted to relive her crimes by looking at her old victims. This is something that male serial killers often do (Holmes, 1996). Furthermore, all four serial killers involved in this research took small items from their victims after each homicide. These items included money, driver's licenses, toys, and such small items as pens. Male serial killers often take small items of jewelry from their victims; but the females in this research did not take jewelry. They were careful to take items that would not be missed, since it was their intention to make the homicide look like a natural death. Simply, noticeable theft was not part of the female multiple murderer's plan. This goes to show that females tend to be very clever, exercising more self-control than males. They are calculating and methodical in their killing, and it would be a mistake to think that just because a killer is a female that she is not as brutal or as calculating as her male counterpart.

**Mindset**

Profiling is an art that involves examining forensic evidence and behavior that is evident at a crime scene. Physical evidence is much easier to interpret than psychological imprints, and so, in order to estimate why an offender engages in certain behaviors, there must be an understanding of what emotional state dominates the individual who commits the crime. Thus, profiling begins with raw emotion because feeling is what drives serial behavior.

Serialists are in search of a particular feeling, most often power over another human being. As they often come from homes devoid of happiness, warmth, and love, serial offenders develop a preconception of how people act. This preconceived notion entails relational hostility and sinister motivations. Simply put, because serial offenders emerge from abusive and unloving environments, the offenders believe that all people will act like the parents and family who were abusive toward the individual. With this expectation of abuse and distrust comes emotional isolation, which manifests itself in the forms of being emotionally flat and failing to feel empathy for others. This is how the mindset of the multiple murderer begins, and when set, it is impossible to change.

Once an understanding of this mindset is created, then behavior can be analyzed. When profiling a case that has been perpetrated by a male offender, a profiler examines how the victim was approached and taken, if the victim was transported, if the victim was restrained and how, if the victim was sexually assaulted and the order in the which the assault took place, what wounds were inflicted and in what order, how the victim was killed, what was done to the body postmortem, what was done at the crime scene, if the body was transported, how the body was dumped or posed, and if there was any contact with the victim's family after the homicide. These are *few* of the highlights that a profiler will examine when analyzing a crime. Whether a victim was brutalized premortem or postmortem is very significant to a profiler, as a sadist is only interested in harming a living victim while a less social-type killer will inflict wounds after the victim is dead. These are two very different types of people, and they will be profiled differently.

The same concepts apply when profiling a female killer. The profiler wants to learn about all of the above questions, but more likely than not, there will be little to no behavior evident at a crime scene where a female serialist has killed. Why? Because females typically use covert methods to murder their victims, and they leave little evidence behind. However, once questions have been raised about a series of deaths and a profiler is called, the profiler should look for several things. This list is a basic questionnaire and should be used as a starting point in an investigation.

## Schurman-Kauflin's 10 Questions

1. Who had access to and was the last person with the victim?
2. Is there one person in particular who is connected with all of the deaths?
3. Is there a person who has the background characteristics relayed in Chapter 4, i.e. abandonment, triad of abuse, animal cruelty, isolation, prevaricator.
4. Who has had stressors within a few weeks of the homicides?
5. Who has kept to herself and been slightly isolated?
6. Who has made verbal statements about hurting or killing?
7. Who has a history of being fascinated by death and torture?
8. Who has been known to tell elaborate untrue stories?
9. Who has been known to volunteer and be helpful to others?
10. Were the homicides committed in a way that resembles profile characteristics listed in Chapter 8, i.e. Crime scene controlled, little evidence, asphyxia, planned.

Once these questions are answered, police may have a better idea as to who may have murdered the victims. At that point, a profiler should work with police to get as much information about the suspect as possible — such as general personality, mindset, attachments, habits, and hobbies. This general picture allows the profiler to construct an investigative plan designed to extract truthful information from the suspect.

For instance, knowing whether a person is an extrovert versus an introvert guides how an interview should be conducted. Introverts do not like being the center of attention and feel less comfortable in crowds than extroverts, who enjoy people. Thus, it would be better to have a one-on-one interview with an introvert because it would be easier to establish rapport in such a setting. An extrovert feels more comfortable with many people, so having two detectives in the room with the suspect would not harm the interview process. The profiler should give detectives tips based on the suspect's personality on how to establish rapport and extract truthful information. A more detailed interview approach is outlined in Chapter 9.

A good profiler can construct an effective investigative and interview strategy that can guide not only the interview but the investigation as well. It should be noted that every suspect should be investigated. Just because a person does not fit a profile does not mean that he or she should not be investigated.

The profile is used to help narrow a suspect pool and garner helpful information. The profiler must be adaptable and willing to work with detectives, no matter direction the case takes. It is essential to be open-minded when it comes to investigating serial crimes, because there is no set rule for who can be a killer.

Case Example

Edna had her first child in 1972. She was a single, African American female who had a penchant for having sex with many men. She was described by those who knew her as uncaring and cold, a person who liked to tell stories to make herself more appealing to potential suitors. Edna was irresponsible and had no family ties to speak of. On her own, she made her way by using men, sleeping her way into rent money. And though she was penniless, she persisted in having children. As a young teenager, she gave birth to a son. Those who knew her said that she was distant and cold to her child, so it was surprising when she had another son by a different father less than two years later. Edna could not hold a steady job, so she was under a great deal of financial pressure. Her stress level was at an all time high when both sons died within a few months of one another. Both died while in Edna's care, when no one else was present. Edna said the boys stopped breathing, and though the oldest child was almost two years old, little suspicion was raised. Instead, both deaths were ruled natural, Sudden Infant Death Syndrome being deemed the culprit.

It wasn't long after her two sons had died when Edna was out and about with several men, drinking and having sex. Accordingly, it didn't take too much time before Edna was pregnant again. Son number three was born to a different father, but before he reached his first birthday, he was found dead. He died in Edn'a care with no one else present. Apparently, he had stopped breathing. Son number three's death was ruled natural; again, SIDS was blamed.

Sympathies ran high for the single woman who was seemingly plagued with misfortune in her life. Three sons had died in her care, and there was seemingly no reason for their deaths. Edna was all alone, poor, and with few friends. She had no family to comfort her, and her money problems were worsening. It was at this point that Edna tried to commit suicide by shooting herself in the stomach. She was found and rushed to the hospital, where a lifesaving procedure spared her. Those surrounding the young woman became worried, so her suicide attempt landed her in the state mental institution where she was treated for depression. In her months of treatment, doctors felt that she was making progress, and less than one year later, Edna was released from the hospital.

Almost as quickly as she closed the door to the state mental institution, Edna was running around with her male companions once more, and she became pregnant by yet a different man. Just like his brothers before him, son number four died before reaching his first birthday. Like the other three deaths, there were no outward signs of trauma to his body, but this was the fourth death to occur in one house. Though SIDS does not run in families, authorities were unmoved by this astonishing coincidence. The fourth death was ruled natural. Edna was free to move on to victim number five.

Life continued for the poor young woman, who continually made her way through a sea of men and beds. She didn't work. She had no ties to family. But she managed to find men who would pay her bills for the luxury of sleeping with her. In 1982, she met a man who fell deeply in love with her and asked her to move in with him and his three children almost immediately. Apparently, Edna didn't like children very much because the very year she moved in with her new beau, one of his children died suspiciously when left in Edna's care. The two-year-old simply stopped breathing, Edna claimed.

Miraculously, the death was ruled natural. SIDS was blamed, and Edna was ready to take on victim number six. The opportunity didn't take long. As fate would dictate, Edna became pregnant again less than a year after victim number five had been buried. Apparently she wasn't too thrilled with the prospect of bringing yet another baby into her life. She found herself a wire coat hanger, fashioned it into a crude instrument, and inserted it into her vagina in a futile attempt to abort the baby. Somehow she managed to carry the baby to term, and she gave birth to her first little girl. Life seemed wonderful for Edna, until a shrewd mental health worker noticed the connection between the five deaths and Edna. Upon his urging, coroners and police examined the deaths more closely and found the coincidence to be too far-fetched. There had been signs to indicate that the deaths were not natural, so Edna was arrested for murder. Seemingly stunned at being caught, Edna admitted to placing a pillow over the fifth victim's face and holding it there for several minutes. When asked why, she simply stated that she wanted the crying child to be quiet.

But Edna would come into a rosy bed of luck, for jurors felt sorry for her (losing five children from her life) and recommended her for the minimum of 10 years in prison. Flabbergasted, police in a neighboring jurisdiction sought prosecution in the deaths of her own sons. The case was proceeding well until the judge refused to allow her recent conviction to be allowed into trial, even though she freely admitted to brutally killing the baby in that case. With no physical evidence and the disallowance of the other case, the charges were dismissed, and Edna served a mere 10 years for killing five children. As of this writing, Edna is free, and in all probability has moved on to victims six, seven, eight, and nine.

Procedure

Applying the Schurman-Kauflin 10 Questions, it would have been impossible to ignore Edna's involvement in the deaths of the children. Whenever law enforcement comes across one or more suspicious deaths, these questions can help focus the investigation and perhaps prevent another death. The following is an example of how the police could have analyzed Edna's situation:

1. Who had access to and was the last person with the victim(s)?

Victim #1: Child asleep in Edna's care when child died.
Victim #2: Child asleep in Edna's care when child died.
Victim #3: Child asleep in Edna's care when child died.
Victim #4: Child asleep in Edna's care when child died.
Victim #5: Edna babysitting for child when child died.

Analysis: Edna had access to each child and was the last person with all the victims.

2. Is there one person in particular who is connected with all of the deaths?

Analysis: Edna was mother to four of the five victims, and she was living with the father of the fifth victim.

3. Is there a person who has the background characteristics related in Chapter 4?

Analysis: Edna came from a broken family, and her father abandoned her when she was very young. She was beaten, raped, and emotionally abused. Her childhood activities consisted of solitary play, and she had a history of emotional outbursts and clinging to teachers.

4. Who has had stressors within a few weeks of the homicides?

Analysis: Edna had been struggling financially since she did not like to work, and in each instance, money had been extremely tight immediately prior to the homicides.

5. Who has kept to herself and been slightly isolated?

Analysis: Edna was described by those who knew her as cold and distant, with a tendency to spend time alone.

6. Who has made verbal statements about hurting or killing?

Analysis: Those who knew her stated that Edna had often discussed killing people.

7. Who has a history of being fascinated by death and torture?

Analysis: Refer to answer #6.

8. Who was known to make up elaborate stories?

Analysis: Edna was described as being emotional and prone to telling wild stories in order to receive attention, primarily from men.

9. Who has been known to volunteer and be helpful to others?

Analysis: Right before the fifth homicide, Edna volunteered to babysit for the children of a close friend. Note that this behavior is consistent with female serial killers who often attempt to gain vulnerable victims by placing themselves in a care-giving role with either children or the sick (and elderly).

10. Were the homicides committed in a way that resembles profile characteristics listed in Chapter 8?

Analysis: In each case, the deaths were covert, meaning that there were no overt signs of homicide. The victims were all overtly helpless and known to one (Edna) individual who was a caregiver. There was little if any evidence present, but there was a pattern of deaths surrounding Edna. The cause of death in the homicides was asphyxiation, which is one of the primary methods female serialists use to kill their victims.

No individual query from the Schurman-Kauflin 10 Questions in and of itself can prove that a person is a serial killer. However, when all ten questions are asked and a background scenario is created, investigators can more easily ascertain whether they are dealing with a strong suspect, which in turn can create interview opportunities. In other words, if police are confident that they are looking at a person who very well could have committed multiple murders, then they can use a profiler to aid in the preparation of an interview designed to illicit information from that specific person.

Obviously, had the Schurman-Kauflin 10 Questions been available when Edna's case was occurring, investigators would have had a better opportunity to question the suspect and gain valuable information.

The questions form the background of a large painting, which is filled in with case and suspect information. Given these details, investigators have a better opportunity to rule in or rule out foul play and/or specific suspects.

# 9

## TORNADO EFFECT

## Motivations

There is one clear motivating factor that drives multiple homicide. Whether it is cloaked by the delivery of horrid mutilation or whether it appears to be a desperate act to gain attention, the root cause is always the same. It's all about control.

## Tornado

Everyone wants power, in a way as individualistic as each separate person appears. To have power is to be safe. Wielding power evinces omnipotence. The degree to which we crave this feeling is dependent upon how we were treated as children. The worse one was treated, the more powerless a person has been made to feel, the more one will fanatically pursue situations of control.

So it should be no surprise that these female killers, these most unusual of human predators, are power-seekers in the most desperate way. By now it should be clear that the home lives of multiple murderers are never what they may appear to be to the outside world. Even if it looks as though the family unit was healthy, there is almost always a malfunction that permanently impairs the killer's ability to function adaptively in life.

Each female recalled feelings of helplessness and hopelessness while growing up, due to abandonment, isolation, and extreme sexual, physical, and emotional abuse. The impetus for violence emerged from a desire to take control of their lives. In other words, the female multiple murderer feels that if she can control and have power over other people, then she can have control over her own life. It's a fine line but one that was seen repetitively.

A female serial killer convicted of three homicides summarizes this mindset concisely.

> All I ever wanted was to be left alone, but nobody would ever do that. There was always somebody there either beating on me or torturing me. If they'd have just left me alone, none of this would ever have happened. Because when I realized that there was nothing I could do about it (the abuse, abandonment), those things in my life, I decided to make a change when I got the chance. And I knew my chance was coming. I knew at some point, the power would come to me. All I had to do was wait it out. There was going to be somebody who was dependent on me for help, and all I had to do was wait. Waiting is kind of like a death. You know it's coming, and it hurts bad. But it's something you have to go through. And after all that waiting, it's finished. I was finished by the time I was through waiting, but I got my chance. I finally had control.

Certain patterns and behaviors were set into motion when these women were very young. From the horrific abuse and emotional cruelty to the intense isolation, the females learned that people were not to be trusted and that self-reliance was the only way to survive. From their early behavioral lessons, they begin a cycle that becomes all consuming and impenetrable by the time they reach adolescence.

This cycle repeats until it is so ingrained that murder becomes inevitable. This is what I have called the Tornado Effect.

## The Tornado Effect

This begins in early childhood when the killer suffers from extreme abuse, emotional detachment, and abandonment. From the terrible events that comprise their lives, the females come to feel helpless, powerless, and it is with the feeling of being without control that the cyclone begins spinning.

At the bottom of the tornado is the condition of being powerless in the face of a terribly abusive situation. This powerlessness leads to feelings of anger and rage. As the condition of powerlessness is contemplated, considered, rage increases. In other words, the female repeatedly thinks about what has been done to her. She recycles it in her head and cannot rid her thoughts of the pain. This leads to increasing feelings of rage, and as the rage grows, a violent fantasy life emerges. The female multiple murderer begins thinking about the act of homicide, though no specific victim is targeted within her mind.

For a while the female simmers, but eventually, another event makes her powerless. The pain returns. Once the killer's thoughts return to the state of powerlessness, rage builds, and the violent fantasies become more specific. Within the fantasies, instead of merely considering how to kill, the female identifies a certain victim. She thinks about whom she could get close to, whom she could control. Then she carefully plans how she would kill that person. In her mind, she rehearses her crime repeatedly until simply imagining the act of murder is not enough to make her calm. Fantasizing no longer makes her feel powerful.

Because her fantasies lose their impact, there is a tendency for the killer to return to the state of powerlessness. She is caught up in feelings of being helpless and out of control. Again, this feeds the feeling of rage, which leads back to the violent fantasy life, and the process expands. Then the next turn of the cyclone is formed.

From fantasy, the female multiple murderer begins acting out. The targets are typically small animals that the female can easily prey upon. Most often, the targets are cats — who, according to the females, are big enough to make them feel powerful but small enough not to hurt them. Eerily, the young killers seek out helpless victims. However, killing animals becomes boring to the female who then begins acting out with other children. Often there is pattern of clinging to other children and picking fights as well. It is as if the young women want their victims to remain close while they hurt them.

Since other children see these young women as outcasts, there is a marked isolation caused by the female's inability to act appropriately, and this leads the female back to the powerlessness state. The cyclone turns again. Once she feels powerless, the rage returns, fantasies grow to the point of detailed plans of murder, but a sense of calm is never restored. So, the female returns to the state of powerlessness.

Examine the cycle:
POWERLESS-RAGE-FANTASY-VIOLENCE-FANTASY-MURDER

When the female has fantasized for years; When the female has killed small animals; When the female torments other children; When the female has done all of the above, then the cycle starts for the first fatal time. From powerlessness, the female moves to rage, and from rage, she moves to detailed murderous thoughts. After she has acted out against small animals and children, it is from here that the next step is taken.

The next step is murder.

However, to the dismay of the female multiple killer, the act of homicide does not stop her from returning to the state of powerlessness, and this creates horrible feelings of stress and anger. Truly she believed that killing would make her feel better. For a brief time, it does, but the powerlessness sneaks back into her thoughts. Because she desires the power that she never had as a young child, a brief feeling of exhilaration and control only momentarily fill her void. Hauntingly, the

# Tornado Effect

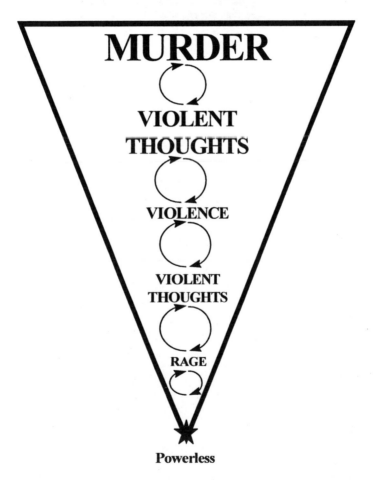

MURDER

VIOLENT
THOUGHTS

VIOLENCE

VIOLENT
THOUGHTS

RAGE

**Powerless**

female's thoughts turn almost immediately to powerlessness after the homicide. Her power fades as the body is found, and her life resumes. In turn, rage emerges, and from rage, the cycle begins again.

Repeatedly, the female's mind returns to each stage, only to build and cycle back once more to the point of committing murder. In essence, it is much like the formation of a tornado, which spins repeatedly and become ever more powerful.

What was remarkable during the interviews with the female killers was the recognition of this sequence. Each woman had an individual story, but the pattern was almost identical from female to female.

POWERLESS-RAGE-FANTASY-VIOLENCE-FANTASY-MURDER

One convicted female serial killer was blunt about how she came to kill. She admitted to killing six people and attempting to kill three others. In this section of the interview, she discussed the process step by step. From the time she was three, all she remembered was violence and trauma, which led to her deviant thoughts.

As a kid, I was just a terror. I mean, when I was a kid, I'd rip things up, the Bible, scream, yell. I would start, and I didn't know how to fight. I'd start it because I was just a mean little kid. If I didn't like you, or if I didn't think I was going to like you, that was the end of you. I think a lot of it had to do with my father beating on me. He'd beat on me, and there was nothing I could do about it. I'd get mad, and any time I got mad, I wouldn't take it out on a person. I'd find the nearest . . . pet. I think that's where a lot of it began. As time went by, every time I got mad, when my father started beating on me, I started in on the cats, and I was like, hey I like this. I guess doing it with animals, I didn't have the power, of hey, I can do this and get away with it. I mean, animals, not too many people care about animals, so the power wasn't there. You know, it wasn't like it was a person. It was like the same all the time. My dad would start, I'd get mad, you know, think about how I could hurt something so I could feel in control, like make a natural high. And it was like then I'd go get a cat, beat it until it didn't get back up on four legs. I know it sounds terrible, but I enjoyed it. As terrible and as bad as it is to say, I was like hey, I can do this and get away with it.

This convicted killer actually recognized her pattern, though she never took steps to stop it. Another convicted mass murderer realized that there were specific "triggers" that led to her murders.

When I reached four or five, I accepted things the way they were. And that's just the way that it was. I knew nothing good was ever going to happen for me. I knew I wasn't like everyone else. Once I left the children's home, you know, I came to reality. I knew my life was ruined. When things, I mean honestly, I was doing things vindictively. I mean there was a purpose to what I was doing. Every time I was raped, I couldn't, I knew my life was ruined. It was like a trigger. I liked to get back at them for what they did to me. I thought about how for a long time. I don't remember too much, a happy memory. I do remember being hit and being held down and raped, and I remember not being able to do any-thing until I got a hold of the cats. When I was strangling them, I mean, I guess that's about the happiest that I can say that I ever was. I remember feeling like I was doing some-thing. I could (see) the cats twitching, and I was feeling good.

The author asked the killer why she felt good when she strangled the cats. She replied "I never was afraid of getting hurt when I was do-ing it, you know what I'm saying? I was the one in control when I was doing the, doing it." She went on to describe how she would think about how to kill human beings, and she said the trigger for her violent thoughts was stress, which made her feel helpless.

Yea, it'd be this or that, you know, whatever (expletive) was going on that day. When I think back on it, uh, you know it was usually something I brought on. You know what I mean? I mean, when, um, I was little, it wasn't my fault, but when I got older, you couldn't stop me from getting into whatever I wanted. And that's what got me into trouble, be-cause it was when I was getting (expletive) that I started thinking, hey, you better stay away from me. I don't need this (expletive), you know? That's when all the fantasies started and I started getting into trouble.

Michelle: A case study

1963 Michelle is born to a prostitute; she is the second of 9 children.
1967 Michelle's natural father gives her and her sister up for adoption.
1968 Michelle endures regular beatings at the hands of her adopted mother.
1968 Michelle stutters and has epileptic seizures.
1969 Neighbors call police because Michelle is being beaten; Michelle and her sister
are removed from the house.
1970 Michelle stalks and kills cats.
1974 Michelle begins dramatic weight gain.
1975 Michelle runs away and begins having sex; runs away to find her natural mother.
1977 Michelle marries and quickly divorces.
1977 Michelle visits local emergency room over 50 times.
1978 Attempts suicide by slashing wrists.
1979 Michelle begins babysitting for money.
1980 Murders two-year-old baby.
1981 Murders four-year-old.
1981 Three days after killing a four-year-old, Michelle kills a two-year-old.
1981 Murders elderly man.
1982 Murders 8-month-old baby.

1982 Murders infant.
1982 Michelle is arrested and pleads guilty to three of the murders.

Michelle was born in a rural, southern town into a poverty-stricken home. Her mother engaged in prostitution while her natural father worked with his hands doing odd jobs. Michelle was the second of nine children, and it was clear from the time that she was born that she was unwanted. Her early years were characterized by sexual and physical abuse from both her mother and father. Even though life was filled with violence, Michelle was devastated when her father was injured in a work-related accident that rendered him unable to work. The family that was struggling, even with the father working, and began to fall apart after the accident. A local church stepped in when Michelle and her sister were given up for adoption. An older church-going couple agreed to take Michelle's sister. However, they wanted nothing to do with Michelle, who was known as a troublemaker. But the only way the couple could adopt Michelle's sister was to take Michelle too, so they did. The couple told Michelle that they didn't want her, and that she had better behave, "or else". The threats were carried out in vicious acts of torment and torture. Michelle was regularly locked in dark closets, beaten, and verbally accosted.

Late one night when her adopted mother was at work, Michelle crept into her sister's room when she heard crying. She found her adopted father nude on top of her sister, and she ran to the phone to call for help. Her adopted father chased her and wrapped the phone chord around her neck until she passed out. The police were repeatedly called to the residence by worried neighbors who watched the sickening abuse. Yet nothing was done to protect the children, and Michelle realized that she was not safe in that house. She began acting out at age seven by stalking little animals in the neighborhood. The preferred targets were cats that Michelle claimed were big enough to make her feel powerful but small enough not to hurt her when she beat and strangled them. This became her favorite Sunday night activity. She also had taken to getting into fights with other children. Teachers stated that Michelle had a bizarre tendency to hang onto other children and that that usually started the fights.

At the same time, Michelle started thinking about what it would be like to wrap her hands around a person's throat. Cats were exciting to her, but they weren't enough to relieve her building stress. She wanted more, the feeling of being all-powerful, and that would only come if she had control over the life of another human being. She had little to no power in her life, so she began eating to make herself feel better, and severe weight gain began. Michelle was becoming greatly obese, and her life was spinning out of control. She was being abused at home, she had never known anything that resembled warmth or love, and she was fantasizing about hurting people. This was too much to take for the young girl, so she began running away. By age twelve she was sneaking out of the house and trying to find her natural mother. After months of attempts, she finally found her mother and moved in with her. This proved to be an almost lethal mistake, as her mother nearly killed her by beating her with a 2x4 board when Michelle made a sarcastic remark to her. Michelle was rushed to a local hospital, where she spent several days, but her mother never came to see her. She said that was the most painful part of that whole incident, that her mother didn't care enough to call or come to see her to make sure that she was all right.

Life became intolerable for Michelle after leaving the hospital. Her mother was erratically violent, and at times, came close to killing Michelle. Each time her mother was abusive, Michelle became convinced that she was ill. She took every opportunity to rush to the emergency room with bizarre ailments, with outrageous claims of being bitten by venomous snakes and suffering from unexplainable red spots. Doctors found no evidence of snake bites or crimson splotches, and hospital staff began to recognize the misfit as a drama queen who craved the attention she received whenever she'd hurry through the emergency room doors. There was a definite pattern that had been established. Being abused. Feeling powerless. Fantasizing about hurting someone. And finally, acting out to feel a sense of control.

Though she was running away and hiding in the hospital whenever she could, life at home was outright miserable. The pattern of acting out was little consolation for the powerlessness and pain that colored her life, so Michelle began wondering what it would be like to kill herself. She thought about all the ways by which she could end it all and escape from the horror in her home. Guns. Knives. Pills. She looked at every possible way to take herself out of this life, and after careful planning, Michelle took a steak knife from the kitchen and slashed it across her wrists. She was found by a family member and taken to the hospital once more. The pattern worked once again.

Michelle had learned that a dramatic lifestyle could make her life more bearable, so she learned to become manipulative and charming with men, who found her sexually easy. Though she was overweight and scarred with acne, there was no shortage of young men who would sleep with her, and she went to bed with virtually anyone who asked. It gave her a sense of power over these typically older men when she lured them into having sex. But the feeling was transitory, and Michelle was left with being pregnant at a very young age. She married a young suitor only to abandon the marriage within a month. Shortly after, she miscarried her baby, and once again, Michelle was left alone with a feeling of helplessness. She began babysitting in the close-knit community where she lived because she was known to love young children. All outside appearances indicated that Michelle was golden with children. They loved having her around, and she would frequently cuddle and rock the children even when she wasn't babysitting. It seemed like the perfect job for Michelle.

Little did the townspeople know that Michelle was a seething caldron of anger. She did enjoy taking care of children, but she also had her fantasies of killing. Whenever she was hurt or stressed, she thought about wrapping her hands around a child's throat. She kept her secret under control until one fateful night in February of 1980. Michelle was looking after a little girl when she couldn't control her fantasies any longer. The young child had fallen and hit her head, and she was screaming in pain. "She wouldn't stop," said Michelle. "I rocked her. I held her, but nothing was working. It was then that I knew she was in trouble." Michelle described holding the young child while sliding her hand around her throat. "I squeezed her. I mean, I know how it sounds, but I squeezed her throat until she didn't move anymore." Michelle also pointed out that she watched the young child's face while she strangled her. "I'm not sure why I did what I did," said Michelle. "But I was like, I can do something no one else can do." It gave her a sense of power.

The young child died at the hospital, and her death was ruled natural. The townspeople grieved, but no one suspected that Michelle was capable of doing such a terrible thing. Instead they comforted her because she was the last one with the baby, and it wasn't long before another parent hired Michelle to care for her child. Michelle was baby-sitting a four-year-old boy when the urge to kill struck again. Her life was spinning out of control. She had no money, and no family to speak of. Men still found her sexually desirable, which led to numerous romps in bed. But no serious relationship ever emerged. Immediately before she was hired to baby-sit for the four-year-old boy, Michelle had been involved in a fight with her then boyfriend. The fight left Michelle feeling helpless and angry, and as the pattern had begun, this led to her violent fantasies. That night, she killed the four-year-old boy by pinching his nose and covering his mouth. "He was happy that night," she recalled. "He wasn't crying or nothing, but I knew he was going to die."

The young child's death was ruled natural, and at Michelle was hired to baby-sit for another young boy while his parents attended the funeral of the child Michelle murdered three days prior. When asked why she decided to kill this boy, Michelle was blunt. "I know how it sounds, but I enjoyed it. I liked watching them die." And she killed the young boy the same way she killed the other. His death was ruled natural, but parents became increasingly nervous about hiring Michelle to baby-sit for their children. Doctors tested Michelle for viruses, which she could be transmitting to the babies. Yet no illnesses were found, and everyone was at a loss as to why this was happening. Parents weren't ready to take any chances, and the babysitting business dried up for Michelle. Out of work and desperate, she convinced an elderly old man that he needed a maid to do the cooking and cleaning in his home. The old man was sickly, filled with cancer and heart disease. Shortly after hiring Michelle, he was found dead on his kitchen floor with a bluish-purple discoloration around his throat. Police believed that he had passed away from his cancer. No autopsy was ordered, and it appeared as if he had died from illness. Little did anyone realize that Michelle's troubles had stressed her to the point of having violent fantasies once more, and she had wrapped a telephone chord around the elderly man's throat "and I pulled on it until he fell down and turned blue." She smiled as she relayed this part of the story and expressed no remorse. "I enjoyed watching police and coroners run around, and I was like hey, I did this and you don't even know." Michelle was very narcissistic. She loved being at the center of controversy, even though suspicion was beginning to arise.

The next incident occurred in 1982. Michelle was asked by her cousin to go with her and her 8-month-old baby girl to the hospital. The child needed her inoculation shots, and during the car ride home from the hospital, the baby cried incessantly. Michelle's cousin stopped at the local convenience store to pick up a toy for the miserable baby who she left in the car with Michelle. However, when she returned to the car, her baby was silent. After examining the child closely, she found that the little girl was not breathing. As Michelle recounts it, "She left me and her in that car, and I don't know what to say. She was crying, and it was like she couldn't stop. I don't exactly know what happened next. The next thing I remember was being in the back seat with my hands on her throat. I don't right know how I got there. It was like a instinct to do what I did."

The child's death was ruled natural, and Michelle was very happy that she was getting away with murder. She made a habit of cutting out newspaper articles and making a scrapbook of her crimes, which she would look at whenever she started fantasizing. "In between Kaitlin* and the last one, I tried my little cousin twice. But he fought me, so I laid off him. I was afraid of getting caught." Her fear of being found out did not supercede her burning desire to kill, and in July 1982, Michelle committed her last murder. The parents of a 10-week-old baby left him in Michelle's care overnight. Michelle was living with a boyfriend in a trailer. The baby was in a crib beside her bed. When her boyfriend awoke the following morning, the baby was dead. Michelle at first claimed that she didn't know what happened, but after a medical examiner determined that the baby had been asphyxiated, Michelle checked herself into a local mental hospital and eventually pled guilty to three of the deaths. She has been in prison for nearly twenty years, but she still has fantasies of killing, which she freely admits.

Though Michelle was described as being slow mentally, she was smart enough to see her own pattern. She realized that it was when she was hurt or angry that she fantasized and then killed. This is how the Tornado Effect works. A child is brutalized to the point of being completely powerless. As a result of this, the child becomes hurt, then enraged, but the child is typically too small to strike out. So, the child retreats into a violent mental realm where she is in control. At first, the fantasies are enough to make her feel better, and the stress subsides. However, as time goes on, another incident occurs which makes the child feel powerless. She becomes angry and turns to even more violent fantasies, which become less and less effective for dealing with stress. Eventually, the child moves beyond the fantasies with each cycle, and she strikes out against small animals. For a while, killing small cats or dogs relieves her stress. But there is always another incident that makes the child feel helpless. This leads to the violent fantasies, killing animals, more violent fantasies, and finally murder. With each time that the child goes through the cyclone of helplessness, rage, violent thoughts, and violence, the child must do more in the fantasies and to the victims in order to relieve stress. It is like a reduced tolerance to alcohol or drugs. A person must do more to achieve the same feeling of exhilaration. This is the tornado effect.

# 10

## INTERVIEWING MULTIPLE MURDERERS

Interviewing multiple murderers is not easy. It is a skill that one develops through work. There are a few tips that aided in this research, and they should be employed in any interview situation. They not only will help extract meaningful information, but they will make the process much more relaxing.

Like the F.B.I.'s study consisting of in-depth interviews with male multiple murderers, this research centered on the offenders themselves, their thoughts, and how they viewed their crimes. By interviewing the offenders, a researcher not only receives the verbal communication but the nonverbal signals as well. This allows the interviewer greater insight into the convicted killer's mind, as she can pinpoint the exact moment when the offender becomes uncomfortable, and can assess the verbal information that follows the subtle indications of stress. It is important to gauge how much responsibility the offenders would acknowledge in prison versus when they were being investigated, because how the offender thinks impacts how she responds to police officers when being questioned.

However, before interview technique can be discussed, the interviewer must first get the offender to agree to an interview. Though this may seem simplistic, it is very difficult and can take years to accomplish. This author has conducted interviews with both male and female multiple murderers; therefore there is a basis for the following statements. Male multiple killers are *much* more agreeable to being interviewed than females. This is a plain fact, and probably one of the main reasons that the author was the only person able to conduct at-length interviews with female offenders for this research. With males, a simple letter stating credentials and the purpose of the research was sufficient to garner the interview. On the other hand, with females, it took years of writing specific letters to each individual in order to even get a response. Each woman was extremely suspicious and unwilling to be part of any research. It was only after writing for over a year or more that these women agreed to be interviewed. It is this author's suggestion that in order to gain compliance an interviewer should be concise in the letters, state the purpose clearly, and maintain professionalism at all times. Do not become personal with the offenders. They will attempt to manipulate you.

These are some steps that an interviewer should take before and during an interview:

- Do a background check
- Set the tone
- Establish rapport
- Guide the interview

**Tailor the Interview Tone Based on Offender's Background**

Prior to sitting down with the offender, the interviewer must obtain as much background information about the offender as possible. Topics that the interviewer should know by memory include the crimes committed, the offender's general personality, and what type of environment the offender came from.

First, in order to have a better understanding of the person, the interviewer should become familiar with the offender's crimes. This can be accomplished by reading newspaper accounts, trial transcripts, interviewing police, and interviewing medical examiners. By having an in-depth knowledge of the crimes, the interviewer shows the offender that she is serious about the interview and has invested the time and energy it takes to learn about an individual.

Second, the interviewer must have some understanding of the offender's general personality. Is the individual an introvert or an extrovert? Does he hate women? Does she hate men? What is the outward persona? To become acquainted with this, an interviewer should attempt to interview an offender's family, friends, and coworkers in order to paint a psychological portrait — before entering the interview. In learning about the personality, the interviewer will have a better comprehension of how to begin the questioning process. For instance, if the offender is an introvert, the interviewer will have to spend more time ingratiating herself to the offender. It is essential to tailor the interview to the individual's personality.

Finally, it helps the process if the interviewer knows about the offender's home life. Was this person financially well-off, or poor? If the latter, it would be beneficial for the interviewer to dress down for the interview in order to make the offender more comfortable. How the interviewee views the interviewer is crucial to extracting information. Making appearance an issue (something which the offender will concentrate on) is a mistake.

## Rapport

Once the interviewer has background knowledge about the offender, then she must establish a link with the offender. No one will talk with someone with whom she or he does not feel comfortable. Therefore, it is essential to create a sense of trust.

Trust is established by creating rapport that includes an objective analysis of the offender. In other words, an interviewer cannot be judgmental when dealing with multiple murderers. Though difficult, it is important to communicate an objective persona to the offender. An interviewer must keep eye contact and avoid facial grimacing. No matter how much the offender baits an interviewer with threats or graphic crime details, an interviewer must not react. Often, when interviewing serial killers, the interviewer is targeted by the offender. The individual will attempt to upset the interviewer by disclosing gory details of crimes or even threatening in order to gauge the reaction. A successful interviewer will not respond to these tests. Instead, it is helpful to keep a calm demeanor and take good notes, keeping in mind that the offender is seeking power by trying to manipulate. The offender is seeking a reaction of some kind, and if it is not given, many times the offender will abandon the game.

Once a sense of trust is established, and the offender determines that the interviewer will listen, the process of information exchange begins. The term exchange is used because information is not simply flowing toward the interviewer. The offender is questioning as well, though the queries will be tacit. Simply, the offender constantly gauges and examines the interviewer for any type of response to what is said. If there is a facial change, the offender will note it and recognize a trigger, which may upset the interviewer. This information becomes valuable to the offender because it is then that he or she has insight into the interviewer. Again, it is important to keep a calm and detached demeanor to avoid this.

In order to extract information from the offender, it becomes necessary to probe and be clear with questions. Often, offenders will be eager to share intimate details of their crimes. It is best to quietly listen and take notes while they discuss their crimes and thoughts. Do not interrupt, even when the offender gets off track. Let the offender finish the thought before asking another question. By not interrupting, what is communicated that the offender has control, which makes him or her feel secure.

When discussing the crimes, offenders will often leave out specific parts — typically, very emotional segments of their lives. For instance, one female serial killer recalled every detail of stalking her elderly victim, wrapping a phone chord around his neck, and pulling tightly, but she could not recall seeing his body afterward. This was a commonality in all of her recollections. When faced with this lack of detail, it is best to move forward to other questions, then come back later once greater rapport has been established. Again, this allows the offender to feel a sense of control, which may be effective in extracting the desired information.

In determining how truthful the offender is being, it is helpful to have as much background information as possible. That way, if deceitful information is being communicated, the interviewer can challenge the offender with the knowledge gained prior to the interview. Often, an offender will simply smile when caught and continue with the interview. This shows the offender that the interviewer is familiar with the offender and that it will be more difficult to lie.

Whenever faced with an individual who will not admit to the crimes, it has been helpful to talk around the situations. Instead of saying murder, use the term "incident." This removes the emotional charge and judgment out, and again allows the offender to feel more comfortable. If the offender still will not admit to the crimes, then it is useful to discuss the offender's perception of the crimes. When an offender can discuss the murders without having to place him or herself there, then the individual can feel more relaxed and candid, thus allowing for more in-depth extraction.

**Author:**

So when you were, you know, ready to do this thing, what was going through your head?

**Convicted serial killer:**

All I knew was that I was gonna do this thing, and there wasn't anybody gonna stop me. I thought about it a lot, how I was gonna do it. The first one, the one I was charged with, I watched her sleeping before I . . . her mouth was open, and I put my hand over like this (displays putting her hand over the girl's nose and mouth). It was warm, you know, her breath on my hand. She kicked a couple of times, but I held her down because she was so little. (Pause). I can't remember nothing after that.

**Author:**

So after this was done, did you, what did you do?

**Convicted serial killer:**

I left. I got up and walked away. I didn't touch her, and she was lying there not moving. Her mouth was still open. I . . . left.

**Author:**

Was there anything on her, like marks or anything someone could see?

**Convicted serial killer:**

No (shaking head). I was good at not leaving no marks. It wasn't hard because they was so little. It was like they was sleeping, and all I had to do was . . . that's all I remember.

The female in this interview was convicted of three murders but is linked to six. Note how the term "thing" was used in place of murder. She actually repeated the word "thing" back in her response. This is called "mirroring." Mirroring occurs when two people begin using similar language and body gestures. Once people mirror one another, rapport is established, because people find it easier to relate to those who are similar. When the interviewer and interviewee use the same phrases or words, the interviewer becomes similar to the offender, at least in the offender's mind. If an interviewer finds the offender mirroring, it is a good sign that the process is going well

Finally, once rapport and information extraction is accomplished, it is often beneficial to maintain an open attitude. When rapport has been established, the interviewer should not break it. In other words, although it may be tempting to show feelings once the interview is complete, it is best to maintain the calm, detached demeanor even when leaving. The author has worked with many police officers who have unsuccessfully tried to argue with suspects in order to obtain information, even to the point of shaking fists at the subjects. These tactics do not work. Never. Though it is much more difficult, it is always more fruitful to follow the simple steps outlined above. These are basic steps, but they have been proven successful time and time again.

In summary, before interviewing a multiple murderer, do as much background research as possible. Learn about the crimes, and the suspect's personality and background. Second, make sure a sense of trust and rapport is created. Leave emotions at the door and maintain composure at all times. With offenders who do not want to admit guilt, use less loaded words to describe the crimes. Instead of "murder", use "incident". Do not call the offender a killer. Treat the individual with as much respect as you would expect in your daily life. Otherwise, there will be no rapport, and no useful information will be exchanged.

11

Conclusion And Future of Profiling

## Review

The results of this exploratory research have demonstrated commonalities in the backgrounds of female multiple murderers. Like their male counterparts, the females came from horribly abusive homes where abandonment was common. Furthermore, like male offenders, the females preyed upon small animals prior to killing humans. This early predation was coupled with an intense fantasy life which was brought about by extreme levels of isolation. Like males, females tended to be promiscuous early in life, and they gravitated toward older sex partners. When looking at the childhoods of multiple murderers, there are striking similarities. The marred backgrounds produce human predators who have little, if any, empathy for others. What this means is that the underpinnings of violence do seem to stem from similar sources. These sources are:

- Lack of bonding
- Abandonment
- Inconsistent and harsh discipline
- Physical, emotional, and sexual abuse

Crime scene patterns and profile patterns were prominent. Most female multiple murderers are Caucasian, divorced, overweight, and living in financial straits. Accordingly, they tend to have low self-esteem. They generally are in their early thirties when caught, as opposed to males who typically are a little younger when apprehended. The older age of the female usually allows her to kill for longer periods of time. The serial killers in this study continued murdering for an average of 5.2 years before being apprehended by police. Male serial killers tend to kill over an average of 4.2 years before arrest (Hickey, 1997). On average, females are connected with six murders. They prefer to kill using poisons or asphyxia, using a method that leaves few marks to identify foul play. And the females carefully plan their murders over long periods of time.

Female serial killers tend to drift from job to job, but when they do work, they migrate toward care-giving occupations such as nursing or babysitting. It has been speculated that female serial killers intentionally gravitate toward these jobs, which place them in a position of power over a helpless person (Kirby, 1998). Being in charge of a helpless group allows easy access to defenseless individuals. This reflects on the female serial killer's planning and her own need to be in control. She selects victims who are helpless because they are easy to assault without leaving physical injury, and if ill, the victim is more likely to be ignored or written off as a natural death.

For instance, the death of an elderly person in a nursing home may go unnoticed because an elderly person is expected to die. Within this study, on average, police did not know that a serial killer was operating until five victims had died. Detection typically occurred during an autopsy that indicated homicide as the manner of death. It was only then that police were alerted to the possibility that someone could be serially killing victims.

The typical crime scene of a female serial killer is to be one with little physical evidence. There will be a helpless victim who passes seemingly without incident. Investigators may find one individual who has some ties to each victim, and often, when female, she will be a care-giver with a history of unsteady employment. It would be prudent to determine whether that female is married, whether she has or is known to have had an interest in death and/or the police, is known to enjoy time alone with helpless individuals, and spends a great deal of time separated from others.

For female mass murderers, instead of occupations involving care giving, there is a pattern of unemployment. At the time of arrest, none of the females convicted of mass murder were legally employed. Unlike female serial killers, the mass murderers use obvious methods of mur-der when they kill their victims. Typically the weapon used is brutal and extremely lethal. A gun is the weapon of choice, followed by knives and cars (used to run over victims).

Female mass murderers model their male counterparts who kill using overt methods, and for men, gun is the weapon of choice. Appre-hension of mass murderers is usually much easier than finding a serial killer because almost always, the mass murderer remains at the death scene or near the immediate area, and typically, there is little to no ef-fort to hide identity.

Having this information can greatly help law enforcement officials who are handling equivocal (questionable) deaths or a series of covert homicides. With this crime scene data and background information, police will be better equipped and more likely to realize that a human predator is at large.

## Can We Cure Them?

Because these individuals failed to bond early and have retreated into a violent fantasy world, it appears as if there is no treatment for their behavior other than incarceration. Though it may sound dismal, no amount of therapy will stop a multiple murderer who has killed from killing again. From interviewing these offenders, it became obvious that after decades of incarceration, these killers still have fantasies of killing, and they freely admit that they would murder again if released.

The futile nature of treatment leaves society with one option, and that is intervention prior to offending. This is why identifying potential warning signs is so important. If these individuals can be treated before they offend, perhaps they will not commit murder. However, it must be noted that there is a question of *when* intervention would be appropriate and what *type* would be helpful.

Clearly, the earlier the intervention, the better. That would be the answer. Once a child is ruined, it is difficult if not impossible to change the person. It is like building a house without creating a support structure. The house may look all right from the outside, but at any moment, the house could crumble. This is a good description of the multiple murderer. If those support systems (love, caring, bonding) are not put into place early in life, the person (house) will eventually crumble.

## Profiling

When faced with a multiple killer who is a female, the aforementioned characteristics may help narrow a field of suspects and provide insight into a killer's mind. This is what profiling is all about. It involves painting portraits of a person's social, psychological, and economic background, and when a competent profiler is used, an investigation can become much easier. A good profiler can assist in the following ways.

## 1. Criminal Profile:

— COMPOSITE OF AN OFFENDER'S

*Age, Sex, Race, Marital Status, Living Arrangement, Employment, Personality, Children, Vehicle Education, Habits, Appearance, Family life, Etc.*

## 2. Investigative Strategy:

— WHEN SUBJECT IS UNKNOWN
*Tips to attempt to "flush out" an unknown subject*
*Tips on how to steer a subject to a certain area for surveillance*

— WHEN SUBJECT IS KNOWN
*How to effectively interview a subject and his/her family, friends, co-workers*
*How to set up an interview room. Pictures, demeanor, time of day, day of week etc.*
*How to proceed with the investigation with this specific subject.*
*Media advice — how to handle the media and how to create a situation that makes the true offender likely to feel nervous and more prone to confess*
*Background information on serial and mass murderers, stalkers, etc. This can aid in the background investigation of a subject.*

## 3. Trial Strategy:

— How to effectively question witnesses on the stand
— In what order to call witnesses

— Who should be in the courtroom

On more than one occasion, this author has been told that the profiling service provided was invaluable. In response to the great number of emails, letters, and phone calls received, I have created a short list of qualifications that a good profiler should have. An expert must possess the following:

1. Extensive study of multiple murder and its motivations.

2. Ph.D. or at least a Master's Degree in Criminal Justice, Psychology, or Sociology.

3. Some homicide investigative experience.

4. Training/mentoring in profiling techniques by a recognized expert.

5. Original research on multiple murder (first-hand experience with these killers is best).

In this author's experience, if an individual does not possess these qualities as a basis, that person is not an expert in multiple murder. Many people make the mistake of thinking that because multiple murderers are often in the popular media that they would be easy to study. Nothing could be further from the truth. These killers are difficult to work with, and the subject matter is dark.

Because criminal profiling is relatively new (in the scope of history), this author cautions law enforcement to perform background checks on all references provided by any expert who may consult. Look for the qualifications posted above. Without them, arguably, one is not an expert.

With that said, criminal profiling is a useful tool that can help solve a case. A good profiler gives direction, elucidates difficult subjects, predicts behavior, aids in investigative techniques, provides interview suggestions, and helps in court situations.

Because of the benefits of profiling, and because there are few consultants who can add so much value, from start to finish, the question is often raised whether computers could be used to predict behavior. Computer-assisted profiling has been discussed for years, but it has never been quite reliable enough to justify complete use. There are many reasons that computers cannot be profilers.

To begin with, personal experience has led the author to believe that there are some things that computers simply cannot do. So much of profiling involves not only insight into physical evidence but intuition as well. An individual's years of experience provide an instinct or "gut" reaction to a crime that is strikingly absent from artificial intelligence. This is not to say that profiling involves psychic phenomenon. It simply means that a person is a better judge of human nature than a computer.

Second, beyond providing composites of likely offenders, profilers give advice on investigative and interview techniques; they conduct the interviews, testify in court, and aid prosecutors with courtroom staging. Again, a computer is left far short when considering the complete package offered by a human profiler. Perhaps this will change one day, and with the amazing abilities of computers, it probably wouldn't be surprising. But for now, the profilers are better equipped to handle multiple murder investigations than the wonderful machines that sit perched on our desks or on our laps.

Multiple murderers are a terrifying threat to our society. From the Ted Bundys of the world to the Oklahoma City bomber, to the most famous female serial killer Aileen Wuornos, these human predators are trolling for victims. For that reason, it is imperative that we all educate ourselves about what we can do to be protected. This is why criminal profiling will be used more and more in the future. There will be a greater awareness concerning what profiling can do for a case because the number of unsolved murders is growing each and every day, and police truly wish to solve these cases. Consider the number of female

219

offenders who until recently have been ignored. Frighteningly, female and child perpetrators will come to the forefront because they are growing in number and cannot be ignored. Though some people may believe that profiling is akin to witchcraft, everyone should be aware that multiple killers are out there, whether male or female. To be forewarned is to be forearmed.

# BIBLIOGRAPHY

Abel, E. L. (1986). Childhood homicide in Erie County, New York. *Pediatrics, 77* (5), 709-713.

Adler, F. (1975). *Sisters in crime.* New York: McGraw Hill.

Alabama man held in killing of 3 workers. (1999, August 6). *Cincinnati Enquirer*, p. A2.

Artingstall, K. A. (1995). Munchausen Syndrome By Proxy. *F.B.I. Law Enforcement Bulletin, 8*, 5-11.

Becker, H.S. (1963). *Outsiders: Studies in sociology.* New York: The Free Press.

Bernardez-Bonesatti, T. (1978). Women and anger: Conflicts with aggression in contemporary women. *Journal of the American Medical Women's Association, 33*, 215-219.

Black, R. (1983). Crime and social control. *American Sociological Review, 48*, 34-45.

*Black's Law Dictionary.* (5th ed.). (1996). Chicago, IL: University Press.

Blackburn, R. (1969). Personality types among abnormal homicides. *British Journal of Criminology, 11*, 1-8.

223

Block, C.R. (1985). Lethal violence in Chicago over seventeen years known to the police, 1965-1981. Chicago, ILL.: Criminal Justice Information Authority.

Boros, S. J. & Brubaker, L. C. (1992). Munchausen Syndrome By Proxy: Case accounts. *F.B.I. Law Enforcement Bulletin,* 6, 16-22.

Bowlby, J. (1944). Forty-four juvenile thieves: Their characters and home life. *International Journal of Psycho-Analysis,* 25, 19-52.

Bowlby, J. (1979). *The making and breaking of affectional bonds.* New York: Routledge Publishing.

Brittain, R. P. (1970). The sadistic murderer. *Medicine, Science and the Law,* 10, 198-207.

Brooks, P., Devine, M., Green, T., Hart, B., & Moore, M. (1988). Serial murder: A criminal justice response. *Police Chief,* 54 (6), 37-45.

Browne, A. (1987). *When battered women kill.* New York: MacMillan.

Browne, A. & Williams, K. (1989). Exploring the effect of resource availability on the likelihood of female perpetrated homicides. *Law and Society Review,* 23, 75-94.

Bunch, B. J., Foley, L.A. and Urbina, S. P. (1983). The psychology of violent female offenders: A sex-role perspective. *The Prison Journal,* 63, (2), 66-79.

Bureau of Justice Statistics. (1998). Criminal victimization 1997: Changes 1996-1997 with trends 1993-1997. (No. 173385). Washington, D.C.: U.S. Department of Justice.

Burgess, A.. (1991). *Rape and sexual assault III: A research handbook.* New York: Garland Publishing.

Burgess, A., Hartman, R., Ressler, R., & Douglas, J. (1986). Sexual homicide: A motivational model. *Journal of Interpersonal Violence,* 1, 251-272.

Bursten, B. (1972). The manipulative personality. *Archives of General Psychiatry,* 26, 318-321.

Cameron, D. & Frazer, E. (1987). *The lust to kill: A feminist investigation of sexual murder*. Washington Square, New York: New York University Press.

Canter, D. (1994). *Criminal shadows: Inside the mind of a serial killer*. London: Harper Collins.

Caputti, J. (1987). *The age of sex crime*. Bowling Green, Ohio: Bowling Green State University Popular Press.

Cichetti, C. (1997, December 2). Murder in the heartland. *Cincinnati Enquirer*, p.1.

Cleckley, H. (1981). *The mask of sanity.* (5^th ed.). Atlanta, GA: Emily S. Cleckley.

Cluff, J. (1997). Feminist perspectives on serial murder: A critical analysis. *Homicide Studies:* 1 (3), 291-308.

Cronin, T. (1996). Criminal personality profiling. Lecture at Northwestern University Traffic Institute, Chicago, Illinois.

Cutrona, C. (1984). Social support and stress in the transition to parenthood. *Journal of Abnormal Psychology*, 91, 378-390.

Darke, J. L. (1990). Sexual aggression: Achieving power through humiliation. In W. L. Marshall, D. R. Laws, & H. E. Barbaree (Ed.), *Handbook of sexual assault: Issues, theories, and treatment of the offender* (pp. 55-72). New York: Plenum.

Decker, S. (1993). Exploring victim-offender relationships in homicide: The role of individual and event characteristics. *Justice Quarterly*, 10, (4), 585-612.

DeRiver, J. (1958). *Crime and the sexual psychopath*. Springfield, Ill: C.C. Thomas.

Dietz, P. (1986). Mass, serial and sensational homicides. *Bulletin of the New York Academy of Medicine*, 62, 477-491.

DiMaio, V. (1998). Practical Homicide Investigation Seminar. Columbus, Ohio.

Dodge, R. W. (1988). The seasonality of crime victimization. Washington, D.C.: U.S. Department of Justice.

Dodge, R. W. & Lentzer, H.R. (1980). Crime and seasonality. Washington, D.C.: U.S. Department of Justice.

Egger, S. A. (1997). *The killers among us.* Upper Saddle River, NJ: Prentice Hall.

Egger, Steven A. (1985). Serial murder and the law enforcement response. *Dissertation Abstracts International, 47,* (University Microfilms No. 1069A)

Ehrhardt, E. (1997). Victimization risks and routine activities: A theoretical examination using a gender-specific and domain-specific model. *American Journal of Criminal Justice, 22* (1), 41-70.

Empey, L. T. (1978). *American delinquency.* Homewood, IL.: Dorsey Press.

Federal Bureau of Investigation. (1959-94). *Crime in America: Uniform crime reports.* Washington, D.C.: United States Government Printing Office.

Flor-Henry, P. (1980). Cerebral aspects of the orgasmic response: normal and deviational. In R. Forbes and W. Pasini (Eds.), *Medical Sexology,* ( pp. 256-262). The Third International Congress. Littleton, MA: PSG Publishing Company.

Flowers, R. B. (1987). *Women and criminality: The woman as victim, offender, and practitioner.* Westport, CT: Greenwood Press, Inc.

Fonagy, P., Target, M. Steele, M., Steele, H., Leigh, T., Levinson, A., & Kennedy, R. (1997). Morality, disruptive behavior, borderline personality disorder, crime and their relationship to security of attachment. In Leslie Atkinson *Attachment and psychopathology (Ed).* pp. 328-357. New York: Guilford Press.

Formby, W. A. (1986). Homicides in a semi-rural southern environment. *Journal of Criminal Justice, 9,* 138-151.

Fox, J. & Levin, J. (1994). *Mass murder.* New York: Berkely Books.

Gazzaniga, M.S. (1985). *Discovering the networks of the mind.* New York: Basic Books.

Geberth, V. (1998). Practical homicide investigation. Lecture at Public Agency Training Council. Indianapolis, Indiana.

Geberth, V. (1996). *Practical homicide investigation* (3rd ed.). Boca Raton, FL: CRC Press.

Goetting, A. (1988). Patterns of homicide among women offenders. *Journal of Interpersonal Violence, 3,* 3-20.

Goetting, A. (1989). Patterns of marital homicide: A comparison of husbands and wives. *Journal of Comparative Family Studies, 2,* 341-354.

Gosselin, C., & Wilson, G. (1984). Fetishism, sadomasochism and related behaviors. In K. Howells (Ed.), *The psychology of diversity,* ( pp. 89-110). Oxford, England: Newport Publishing.

Groth, N. (1979). *Men who rape.* New York: Plenum Press.

Gunmen outlined "big kill" in diary. (1999, April 25). *Cincinnati Enquirer,* p. 1.

Hagerty, W. (1997). Deviant sexual behavior and other related activity. Lecture at the Institute of Police Technology and Management. Nashville, Tennessee.

Hare, R. (1993). *Without conscience: The disturbing world of psychopaths among us.* New York: Pocket Books.

Hartl, E. M. Monnelly, E. P., and Elderkin, R.D. (1982). *Physique and delinquent behavior.* New York: Academic Press.

Hartman, M.S. (1977). *Victorian murderesses: A true history of thirteen respectable French and English women accused of unspeakable crimes.* New York: Schocken Books.

Hawkins, D.F. (1986). Black and white homicide differentials: Alternative to inadequate theory. In Darnell F. Hawkins (Ed.), *Homicide Among Black Americans.* Lanham, MD: University Press of America.

Hazelwood, R., Dietz, P., & Warren. J. (1992). The criminal sexual sadist. *F.B.I. Law Enforcement Bulletin, 59,* (2), 12-20.

Hickey, E. (1991). *Serial murderers and their victims.* Belmont, CA: Wadsworth.

Hickey, E. (1997). *Serial murderers and their victims* (2nd ed.). Belmont, CA: Wadsworth Publishing.

Holmes, R. (1999). Personal Interview. Louisville, Kentucky.

Holmes, R., & Holmes, S. (1998). *Serial murder* (2nd ed.). Thousand Oaks, CA: Sage Publications.

Holmes, S., Hickey, E, & Holmes, R. (1991). Female serial murderesses: Constructing differentiating typologies. *Journal of Contemporary Criminal Justice* 7 (4), 245-256.

Holmes, R. (1989). *Profiling violent crimes: An investigative tool.* Newbury Park, CA: Sage Publications.

Holmes, R., & Holmes, S. (1994). *Murder in America.* Thousand Oak, CA: Sage Publications.

Holmes, R., & Holmes, S.T. (1996). *Profiling violent crimes: An investigative tool.* 2nd Ed. Thousand Oaks, CA: Sage Publications.

Holmes, Ronald M. (1996). Lecture at The Scientific Study of Death. Louisville, Kentucky.

Holmes, R. & DeBurger, J. E., (1985). Profiles in terror: The serial murderer. *Federal Probation*, September,. 29-34.

Hooton, E. (1939). *Crime and the man.* Cambridge, MA: Harvard University Press.

Horney, K. (1945). *Our inner conflicts.* New York: Norton Publishing.

Jackson, J., & Bekerian, D. (1997). *Offender profiling: Theory, research and practice.* New York: John Wiley and Sons.

Jones, A. (1980). *Women who kill.* New York, New York: Holt, Rinehart and Winston.

Jurik, N.C. & Winn, R. (1990). Gender and homicide: A comparison of men and women who kill. *Violence and Victims*, 5 (4), 227-242.

Kaplun, D. & Reich, R. (1976). The murdered child and his killers. *American Journal of Psychiatry*, 133 (7), 809-813.

Keeney, B. T., & Heide, K. (1994). Gender differences in serial murderers: A preliminary analysis. *Journal of Interpersonal Violence*, 9 (3), 383-398.

Kelleher, M. (1997). *Flashpoint: The American mass murderer.* Westport, CT: Praeger Publishing.

Keppel, R. (1997). *Signature killers.* New York: Pocket Books.

Kirby, P. (1998). The feminization of serial killing: A gender identity study of male and female serialists using covert methods of murder. *Dissertation Abstracts International*, 9842482 (University Microfilms No. 98424482)

Kowalski, G. S., Shields, A. J., & Wilson, D. G. (1985). The female murderer: Alabama 1929-1971. *American Journal of Criminal Justice*, 10 (1), 75-90.

Kraft-Ebbing, R. V. (1901). *Psychopathia sexualis, with especial reference to the antipahtetic sexual instinct: A medico-forensic study.* Aberdeen: Aberdeen University Press.

Lane, B. & Gregg, W. (1995). *The encyclopedia of serial killers.* New York: Berkley Books.

Lemert, E. (1951). *Social pathology.* New York: McGraw-Hill Publishers.

Levin, J. & Fox, J. A. (1985). *Mass murder: America's growing menace.* New York: Plenum.

Levin, J. & Fox, J. A. (1991). *Mass murder: America's growing menace* (2nd ed.). New York: Plenum.

Lester, D. (1995). *Serial killers: The insatiable passion.* Philadelphia, PA: Charles Press Publishers, Inc.

Leyton, E. (1986). *Compulsive killers: The story of multiple murder.* New York: New York University Press.

Lindsay, P. (1958). *The mainspring of murder.* London: John Lang.

Lombroso, C. (1911). *Crime, its causes and remedies.* Heinemann, London.

MacDonald, J. M. (1995). *Rape: Controversial issues.* Springfield, ILL: Charles C. Thomas Press.

Mann, C.R., (1996). *When women kill.* Albany, NY: State University of New York Press.

Mawson, A. R., & Mawson, C.D. (1977). Psychopathy and arousal: A new interpretation of the psychophysiological literature. *Biological Psychiatry*, 12, 49-74.

McClain, P.D. (1982-83). Black females and lethal violence: Has time changed the circumstances under which they kill? *Omega*, 13, 479-585.

McCord, W., & McCord, J., & Irving, K. (1959). *Origins of crime: A new evaluation of the Cambridge-Comerville youth study.* New York: Columbia University Press.

Megargee, E.I. (1966). Undercontrolled and overcontrolled personality types in extreme antisocial aggression. *Psychol. Monogr.* 80, Whole No. 611.

Meloy, J. R. (1988). *The psychopathic mind.* Northvale, NJ: Jason Aronson Publishers.

Norris, J. (1988). *Serial killers.* New York: Bantam Books.

Ogle, R., & Maier-Datkin, D., & Thomas, B. J. (1995). A theory of homicidal behavior among women. *Criminology*, 33, (2), 173-193.

Owen, D. R. (1972). The 47 XYY male: A review. *Psychological Bulletin*, 78, 71.

Palermo, G. B. (1997). The berserk syndrome: A review of mass murder. *Aggression and Violent Behavior*, 2, (1), 1-8.

Parisi, N. (1982). Exploring female crime patterns. In E.P.N. Rafter & E. Stanko (Eds.), *Judge, lawyer, victim, thief; women, gender roles, and criminal justice*, (pp. 111-129). Boston: Northeastern University Press.

Patton, M. Q. (1990). *Qualitative evaluation and research methods.* (2^nd ed.). Newbury Park, CA: Sage.

Pearson, E. (1946). Rules for murderesses. In Will Cuppy (Ed.) *Murder without tears.* New York: Sheridan House.

Petee, T. A., Padgett, K. G. & York, T. S. (1997). Debunking the stereotype: An examination of mass murder in public places. *Homicide Studies,* 1 (4), 317-337.

Pettys, D. (1999, August 1) Mass killer's wife had safety concerns, sister says. *Cincinnati Enquirer.* P. A8.

Pokorny, A.D. (1965). A comparison of homicides in two cities. Journal of *Criminal Law, Criminology, and Police Science,* 56, 479-487.

Polk, K., & Schaefer, W. E. (1972). *Schools and delinquency.* Englewood Cliffs, N.J.: Prentice-Hall Publishers.

Pollak, O. (1950). The criminality of women. Philadelphia, PA: University of Pennsylvania Press.

Prentky, R., Burgess, A., Rokous, A., Hartman, C., Resler, R., & Douglas, J. (1989). The presumptive role of fantasy in serial murder. *American Journal of Psychiatry,* 146 (7), 887-892.

Reich, W. (1945). *Character analysis.* New York: Farrar, Straus, & Giroux.

Resnick, P. J. (1969). Child murder by parents. *American Journal of Psychiatry,* 126(3), 325-334.

Ressler, R, Douglas, J. & Burgess, A. (1988). *Sexual homicide: patterns and motives.* Lexington, MA; Lexington Books.

Ressler, R. (1985). Crime scene and profile characteristics of organized and disorganized murderers. *F.B.I. Law Enforcement Bulletin,* 54, 18-25.

Rojeck, D. G. (1996). Changing homicide patterns. NIJ research report: The nature of homicide: Trends and changes. *U.S. Department of Justice,* 106-113.

Riedel, M., & Rinehart, J. (1996). Getting away with murder: An examination of arrest clearances. *National Institute of Justice Research Report,* 91-98.

Rose, L. (1986). *Massacre of the innocents: Infanticide in Great Britain 1800-1939.* London, U.K.: Routeledge and Degan Paul.

Rothstein, A. (1980). *The narcissistic pursuit of perfection.* New York: International Universities Press.

Rule, A. (1980). *The stranger beside me.* New York: Norton Publishing.

Sade, Marquis de. (1797). *Les infortunes de la vertu.* Charenton: Sade.

Sampson, R.J. (1987). Personal violence by strangers: An extension and test of the opportunity model of predatory victimization. *Journal of Criminal Law and Criminology, 78,* 327-356.

Sampson, R.J., & Wilson, W. J. (1995). Toward a theory of race, crime, and urban inequality. In J. Hagan & R. Peterson (Eds.), *Crime and inequality* (pp. 37-54). Stanford, CA: Stanford University Press.

Schlesinger, L. B. & Revitch, E. (1980). Stress, violence and crime. In I. L. Kutash & L. B. Schlesinger (Eds.), *Handbook on stress and anxiety.* San Francisco: Jossey-Bass.

Sears, D. J. (1991). *To kill again: the motivation and development of serial murder.* Wilmington, DE: Scholarly Resources, Inc.

Sheldon, W. (1940). *The varieties of human physique: An introduction to constitutional psychology.* New York: Harper & Row Publishers.

Silver, C.R., & Kates, D. B. (1979). Self-defense, handgun ownership, and the independence of women in violent sexist society. In D. B. Kates (Ed.), *Restricting handguns: The liberal skeptics speak out* (pp. 75-90). Croton-on-the Hudson, NY: North River Press.

Silverman, R.A. & Kennedy, L.W. (1987). *The female perpetrator of homicide in Canada.* Edonton, Alberta: Centre for Criminological Research.

_____(1988). Women who kill their children. *Violence and Victims,* 3 (2), 113-127.

Silverman, R. A. & Kennedy, L. W. (1995) Uncleared homicides in Canada and the United States. NIJ research report: Lethal violence. U.S. Department of Justice: 81-85.

Skrapec, C. (1997). Serial murder: motive and meaning. *Dissertation Abstracts International,* (University Microfilms No. A-9808004)

Smart, C. (1976). *Women, crime and criminology: A feminist critique.* London: Routeledge and Kegan Paul.

Smith, D., & Over, R. (1987). Male sexual arousal as a function of the content and the vividness of erotic fantasy. *Psychophysiology, 24,* 334-339.

Steffensmeier, D. (1980). Sex differences in patterns of adult crime 1965-77. *Social Forces,* 58, 344-357.

Straus, M. L. (1986). Domestic violence and homicide antecedents. *Bulletin of the New York Academy of Medicine,* 62 (5), 446-465.

Sykes, G. M. & Matza, D. (1957). Techniques of neutralization: A theory of delinquency. *American Sociological Review* , 22, 667-669.

Totman, J. (1978). *The murderers: A psychosocial study of criminal homicide.* San Francisco, CA: R and E Research Associates.

Van Hoffman, E. (1990). *A venom in the blood.* Crawfordsville, IN: Connelley & Sons.

Ward, D.A., Jackson, M., & Ward, R. E.(1969). Crimes of violence by women. In Donald Mulvihill (Ed.), *Crimes of Violence.* (pp. 864-889). Washington, DC: U.S. Government Printing Office.

Weis, J. (1976). Liberation and crime: The invention of the new-female criminal. *Crime and Social Justice,* 6, 17-27.

Weisheit, R. (1986). When mothers kill their children. *The Social Science Journal,* 23 (4), 439-448.

Wilbanks, W. (1982). Murdered women and women who murder: A critique of the literature. In N. Rafter and E. Stanko (Eds.), *Judge, lawyer, victim, thief: Women, gender roles, and criminal justice.* (pp. 151-180). Boston: Northeastern University Press.

Wilson, J. & Herrnstein, R. (1985). *Crime and human nature.* New York: Simon and Schuster.

Wilson, C. & Seaman, D. (1993). *Encyclopedia of modern murder.* New York: Putnam Publishing.

Wilson, C. & Seaman, D. (1996). *The serial killers: A study in the psychology of violence.* London: W. H. Allen Publishing.

Wolfgang, M. (1958). *Patterns of criminal homicide.* Philadelphia: University of Pennsylvania Press

Wolf, N. (1991). *The beauty myth.* New York: Random House Publishing.

Wood, W. P. (1994). *The bone garden.* New York: Pocket Books.
Yochelson, S. & Samenow, S. (1977). *The criminal personality.* New York: Jason Aronson Publishers.

## Acknowledgments

First and foremost, I would like to thank Dr. Ronald M. Holmes for his foresight and intellect. Dr. Holmes was a guiding force behind my work, and without him it would have been extremely difficult to complete this study.

I also wish to thank the California, Florida, Kentucky, Missouri, and Ohio Departments of Correction.

As a psychologist, my mother, Sharon, was able to provide insight into the deviant mind, teaching me about psychopaths and acting as a sounding board for my ideas. Though she's only now coming to truly understand what serial murder is all about, she was very helpful when I was writing to these offenders.

Finally, I'd like to thank my husband, Jim. He accompanied me when I went around the country to conduct these interviews and he worried every time I went in to meet a multiple murderer. He has always believed that I would be a success in this field, and without him, this would not have been possible. Thank you, all.

# Also from Algora Publishing:

CLAUDIU A. SECARA
*THE NEW COMMONWEALTH*
*From Bureaucratic Corporatism to Socialist Capitalism*

The notion of an elite-driven worldwide perestroika has gained some credibility lately. The book examines in a historical perspective the most intriguing dialectic in the Soviet Union's "collapse" — from socialism to capitalism and back to socialist capitalism — and speculates on the global implications.

IGNACIO RAMONET
*THE GEOPOLITICS OF CHAOS*

The author, Director of *Le Monde Diplomatique,* presents an original, discriminating and lucid political matrix for understanding what he calls the "current disorder of the world" in terms of Internationalization, Cyberculture and Political Chaos.

TZVETAN TODOROV
*A PASSION FOR DEMOCRACY –*
*Benjamin Constant*

The French Revolution rang the death knell not only for a form of society, but also for a way of feeling and of living; and it is still not clear as yet what did we gain from the changes.

MICHEL PINÇON & MONIQUE PINÇON-CHARLOT
*GRAND FORTUNES –*
*Dynasties of Wealth in France*

Going back for generations, the fortunes of great families consist of far more than money— they are also symbols of culture and social interaction. In a nation known for democracy and meritocracy, piercing the secrets of the grand fortunes verges on a crime of lèse-majesté . . . *Grand Fortunes* succeeds at that.

CLAUDIU A. SECARA
*TIME & EGO –*
*Judeo-Christian Egotheism and the Anglo-Saxon Industrial Revolution*

The first question of abstract reflection that arouses controversy is the problem of Becoming. Being persists, beings constantly change; they are born and they pass away. How can Being change and yet be eternal? The quest for the logical and experimental answer has just taken off.

JEAN-MARIE ABGRALL
*SOUL SNATCHERS: THE MECHANICS OF CULTS*

Jean-Marie Abgrall, psychiatrist, criminologist, expert witness to the French Court of Appeals, and member of the Inter-Ministry Committee on Cults, is one of the experts most frequently consulted by the European judicial and legislative processes. The fruit of fifteen years of research, his book delivers the first methodical analysis of the sectarian phenomenon, decoding the mental manipulation on behalf of mystified observers as well as victims.

JEAN-CLAUDE GUILLEBAUD
*THE TYRANNY OF PLEASURE*

Guillebaud, a Sixties' radical, re-thinks liberation, taking a hard look at the question of sexual morals -- that is, the place of the forbidden -- in a modern society. For almost a whole generation, we have lived in the illusion that this question had ceased to exist. Today the illusion is faded, but a strange and tumultuous distress replaces it. No longer knowing very clearly where we stand, our societies painfully seek answers between unacceptable alternatives: bold-faced permissiveness or nostalgic moralism.

SOPHIE COIGNARD AND MARIE-THÉRÈSE GUICHARD
*FRENCH CONNECTIONS –*
*The Secret History of Networks of Influence*

They were born in the same region, went to the same schools, fought the same fights and made the same mistakes in youth. They share the same morals, the same fantasies of success and the same taste for money. They act behind the scenes to help each other, boosting careers, monopolizing business and information, making money, conspiring and, why not, becoming Presidents!

VLADIMIR PLOUGIN
*RUSSIAN INTELLIGENCE SERVICES.* Vol. I. Early Years

Mysterious episodes from Russia's past – alliances and betrayals, espionage and military feats – are unearthed and examined in this study, which is drawn from ancient chronicles and preserved documents from Russia, Greece, Byzantium and the Vatican Library. Scholarly analysis and narrative flair combine to give both the facts and the flavor of the battle scenes and the espionage milieu, including the establishment of secret services in Kievan rus, the heroes and the techniques of intelligence and counter-intelligence in the 10th-12th centuries, and the times of Vladimir.

JEAN-JACQUES ROSA
*EURO ERROR*

The European Superstate makes Jean-Jacques Rosa mad, for two reasons. First, actions taken to relieve unemployment have created inflation, but have not reduced unemployment. His second argument is even more intriguing: the 21st century will see the fragmentation of the U. S., not the unification of Europe.

ANDRÉ GAURON
*EUROPEAN MISUNDERSTANDING*

Few of the books decrying the European Monetary Union raise the level of the discussion to a higher plane. *European Misunderstanding* is one of these. Gauron gets it right, observing that the real problem facing Europe is its political future, not its economic future.

DOMINIQUE FERNANDEZ
PHOTOGRAPHER: FERRANTE FERRANTI
*ROMANIAN RHAPSODY — An Overlooked Corner of Europe*

"Romania doesn't get very good press." And so, renowned French travel writer Dominique Fernandez and top photographer Ferrante Ferranti head out to form their own images. In four long journeys over a 6-year span, they uncover a tantalizing blend of German efficiency and Latin nonchalance, French literature and Gypsy music, Western rationalism and Oriental mysteries. Fernandez reveals the rich Romanian essence. Attentive and precise, he digs beneath the somber heritage of communism to reach the deep roots of a European country that is so little-known.

PHILIPPE TRÉTIACK
*ARE YOU AGITÉ? Treatise on Everyday Agitation*

"A book filled with the exuberance of a new millennium, full of humor and relevance. Philippe Trétiack, a leading reporter for *Elle*, goes around the world and back, taking an interest in the futile as well as the essential. His flair for words, his undeniable culture, help us to catch on the fly what we really are: characters subject to the ballistic impulse of desires, fads and a click of the remote. His book invites us to take a healthy break from the breathless agitation in general." — *Aujourd'hui le Parisien*

"The 'Agité,' that human species that lives in international airports, jumps into taxis while dialing the cell phone, eats while clearing the table, reads the paper while watching TV and works during vacation – has just been given a new title." — *Le Monde des Livres*

PAUL LOMBARD
*VICE & VIRTUE — Men of History, Great Crooks for the Greater Good*

Personal passion has often guided powerful people more than the public interest. With what result? From the courtiers of Versailles to the back halls of Mitterand's government, from Danton — revealed to have been a paid agent for England — to the shady bankers of Mitterand's era, from the buddies of Mazarin to the builders of the Panama Canal, Paul Lombard unearths the secrets of the corridors of power. He reveals the vanity and the corruption, but also the grandeur and panache that characterize the great. This cavalcade over many centuries can be read as a subversive tract on how to lead.

RICHARD LABÉVIÈRE
*DOLLARS FOR TERROR — The U.S. and Islam*

"In this riveting, often shocking analysis, the U.S. is an accessory in the rise of Islam, because it manipulates and aids radical Moslem groups in its shortsighted pursuit of its economic interests, especially the energy resources of the Middle East and the oil- and mineral-rich former Soviet republics of Central Asia. Labévière shows how radical Islamic fundamentalism spreads its influence on two levels, above board, through investment firms, banks and shell companies, and clandestinely, though a network of drug dealing, weapons smuggling and money laundering. This important book sounds a wake-up call to U.S. policy-makers." — *Publishers Weekly*

JEANNINE VERDÈS-LEROUX
*DECONSTRUCTING PIERRE BOURDIEU*
*Against Sociological Terrorism From the Left*

Sociologist Pierre Bourdieu went from widely-criticized to widely-acclaimed, without adjusting his hastily constructed theories. Turning the guns of critical analysis on his own critics, he was happier jousting in the ring of (often quite undemocratic) political debate than reflecting and expanding upon his own propositions. Verdès-Leroux has spent 20 years researching the policy impact of intellectuals who play at the fringes of politics. She suggests that Bourdieu arrogated for himself the role of "total intellectual" and proved that a good offense is the best defense. A pessimistic Leninist bolstered by a ponderous scientific construct, Bourdieu stands out as the ultimate doctrinaire more concerned with self-promotion than with democratic intellectual engagements.

HENRI TROYAT
*TERRIBLE TZARINAS*

Who should succeed Peter the Great? Upon the death of this visionary and despotic reformer, the great families plotted to come up with a successor who would surpass everyone else — or at least, offend none. But there were only women — Catherine I, Anna Ivanovna, Anna Leopoldovna, Elizabeth I. These autocrats imposed their violent and dissolute natures upon the empire, along with their loves, their feuds, their cruelties. Born in 1911 in Moscow, Troyat is a member of the Académie française, recipient of Prix Goncourt.

JEAN-MARIE ABGRALL
*HEALERS OR STEALERS — Medical Charlatans in the New Age*

Jean-Marie Abgrall is Europe's foremost expert on cults and forensic medicine. He asks, are fear of illness and death the only reasons why people trust their fates to the wizards of the pseudo-revolutionary and the practitioners of pseudo-magic? We live in a bazaar of the bizarre, where everyday denial of rationality has turned many patients into ecstatic fools. While not all systems of nontraditional medicine are linked to cults, this is one of the surest avenues of recruitment, and the crisis of the modern world may be leading to a new mystique of medicine where patients check their powers of judgment at the door.

DR. DEBORAH SCHURMAN-KAUFLIN
*THE NEW PREDATOR: WOMEN WHO KILL — Profiles of Female Serial Killers*
This is the *first book ever* based on face-to-face interviews with women serial killers.